D1681033

The Structure of Truth

The Structure of Truth

The 1970 John Locke Lectures

DONALD DAVIDSON

Edited with an introduction by
CAMERON DOMENICO KIRK-GIANNINI
AND ERNIE LEPORE

OXFORD
UNIVERSITY PRESS

OXFORD
UNIVERSITY PRESS

Great Clarendon Street, Oxford, OX2 6DP,
United Kingdom

Oxford University Press is a department of the University of Oxford.
It furthers the University's objective of excellence in research, scholarship,
and education by publishing worldwide. Oxford is a registered trade mark of
Oxford University Press in the UK and in certain other countries

The text by Donald Davidson © Marcia Cavell 1970
Editorial material © Cameron Domenico Kirk-Giannini and Ernie Lepore 2020

The moral rights of the authors have been asserted

First Edition published in 2020

Published in the United States of America by Oxford University Press
198 Madison Avenue, New York, NY 10016, United States of America

British Library Cataloguing in Publication Data
Data available

Library of Congress Control Number: 2019952034

ISBN 978–0–19–884249–1

DOI: 10.1093/oso/9780198842491.001.0001

Contents

Introduction

The Locke Lectures in Context

Much of what follows in these lectures has already been published in one way or another, but what is familiar appears here in a novel form: either reworked from earlier published material or as early drafts which would subsequently appear after revision. In other words, these lectures comprise an invaluable historical document that illuminates how Davidson was thinking about the theory of meaning, the role of a truth theory therein, the ontological commitments of a truth theory, the notion of logical form, and so on, at a pivotal moment in the development of his thought. It is especially fitting that they should appear together in print for the first time in 2020, the fiftieth anniversary of their delivery in 1970.

There was a great deal of excitement surrounding the lectures at the time of Davidson's visit to Oxford. For years, David Wiggins and Michael Dummett (among others) had been regular visitors to the Stanford Philosophy Department, during which time they were essentially Davidson's guests. So, although Davidson had not yet published much prior to his arrival in Oxford, what he had published was both familiar to and quite influential on the philosophers in the community there, including Wiggins, Dummett, John McDowell, and Gareth Evans. Indeed, McDowell recalls Wiggins having all his New College undergraduates read "Actions, Reasons, and Causes" "in fading blue mimeo for a discussion group sometime between 1963 and 1965" (when he was Wiggins's undergraduate pupil), urging them as well to read Davidson's early language papers "Truth and Meaning" and "On Saying That." Another factor contributing to the excitement surrounding Davidson's lectures was that Noam Chomsky had delivered his legendary Locke Lectures just the year before, generating interest in the nature of language. In this context, Davidson's influential "Truth and Meaning" was ripe for scrutiny. After each of the lectures, which took place between May 13 and 29, 1970, philosophers would reassemble at Merton Street to discuss Davidson's project, and Davidson would patiently and carefully respond to

The Structure of Truth: The 1970 John Locke Lectures. Cameron Domenico Kirk-Giannini and Ernie Lepore,
Oxford University Press (2020). © Cameron Domenico Kirk-Giannini and Ernie Lepore.
DOI: 10.1093/oso/9780198842491.001.0001

each critique. Given the reputation of Davidson's work in Oxford even before he arrived, the general excitement there concerning the philosophy of language, and Davidson's willingness to engage in extended discussion with the philosophers attending the lectures, it is perhaps unsurprising that the so-called "Davidsonic Boom" ensued in the early 1970s.[1]

We can locate the roots of many of Davidson's arguments and themes in these lectures and see how they developed in his later essays. There will inevitably be a great deal of interest in charting how the early Davidson conceived of some of the ideas that only appear in later essays—for example, the omniscient interpreter argument, which makes its appearance in Lecture VI. It will be obvious to anyone familiar with Davidson's writings that he is much more forthcoming here than in his published work about what his goal is—namely, to offer a theory of meaning—about why he thinks a truth theory can help to achieve this goal, and about why he thinks there aren't other ways to move forward. This comes out especially clearly in the first and last of the six lectures.

We are quite keen about the publication of these lectures, not so much because we believe that they contain hitherto completely unknown ideas of Davidson's (though there are discussions that have no echo in any of his published works), but rather because they are written so as to be presented to an audience as a fully organized and coherent exposition of his program in the philosophy of language. This kind of programmatic exposition is unique in the Davidsonian corpus. Even the various collections of his essays that have so far appeared fail to offer as coherent a presentation of his major themes, situating them within an overarching program. If these lectures had been widely available at the time, we believe the reception of his work, especially in the philosophy of language, might have been very different. Given the systematic nature of their presentation of Davidson's semantic program, we also hope that they will be of use to those encountering his thought for the first time.

Our intent in this brief introduction is merely to provide an overview of the contents of the lectures and, when relevant, to gesture at how they depart from previously published works. We pay special attention to passages that either have never appeared before in print or appear here in a novel form. What we do not provide, however, is any exegesis or criticism of our own. There are numerous books, collections, and essays in print devoted

---

[1] Special thanks to Chris Peacocke and John McDowell for sharing their recollections of these events.

to these exegetical and critical projects; we refer the reader to the bibliography at the end of the book for further information. In addition to the writing of this introduction, our work as editors of this volume has involved the preparation of the text of the lectures for publication, a search through Davidson's published work to find connections with the material that appears in them, and historical research into the reception of the lectures by those at Oxford when they were delivered. Our investigations uncovered multiple versions of the texts of a number of the lectures.[2] In some of these cases, it was relatively straightforward to identify which version was the latest on the basis of evidence like the correction of typographical errors, and we have followed the text of the latest version; in others, we have simply opted for whichever version of a given passage seems to us clearer. At times the text of the lectures has been corrected; when these changes amount to more than the elimination of typographical errors, material that has been introduced or replaced by us appears in brackets: "[]" (though readers should be aware that Davidson sometimes set off sections of text with brackets in his manuscripts—the difference between editorial insertions and Davidson's own notes should be clear from the length of the material in brackets). We have, however, tried as much as possible to leave Davidson's prose intact. Readers should keep in mind that Davidson's style has been influenced by the fact that the text was prepared to be delivered orally rather than read as a book.

We now turn to the lectures.

Lecture I: Speaking the Truth

Davidson's first lecture begins with an extended defense of the claim that the notion of *speaking the truth* plays a foundational role in semantic theory. What is special about speaking the truth, Davidson claims, is that anyone who is competent with a language and who knows the relevant facts about the world is in a position to know whether a speaker of that language speaks the truth on any given occasion. In this regard, speaking the truth is unique—other linguistic acts, such as *asserting*, cannot be identified solely on the basis of semantic competence and knowledge of the way the world is. For one must determine a speaker's intentions in order to decide whether

---

[2] Special thanks to Anita Avramides and Kirk Ludwig for giving us access to their copies of the lectures, and to Marcia Cavell for supporting the publication of the lectures as a volume.

she is asserting, whereas one need only hear her correctly to know what she has said.

This is not to say that there are no conventional devices associated with linguistic acts such as assertion. The indicative mood is a conventional device which, when employed sincerely, serves to mark a speaker's utterance as an assertion. But any conventional device associated with a linguistic act other than *speaking the truth* can be used without the right intentions, as in mimesis. So, no other linguistic act is as intimately connected to linguistic competence, which is, after all, the object of semantic inquiry.

Our pre-theoretical notion of speaking the truth does not conform exactly to Davidson's claims about it. When a speaker uses metaphor or hyperbole to communicate a truth, we are often inclined to credit her with having spoken the truth. In such cases, one needs to draw on more than one's linguistic competence to decide whether the truth has been spoken. Davidson maintains, however, that there is nonetheless a notion of speaking the truth that is fit to play a foundational role in the theory of meaning. Indeed, Davidson suggests that it is partly our ability to determine whether someone speaks the truth in his favored sense that enables us to determine whether she speaks the truth in using metaphorical or hyperbolic language.

Having introduced the notion of speaking the truth and argued for its importance in semantic theory, Davidson proceeds to clarify that he is not in the business of offering an *analysis* of meaning. Indeed, he believes that the project of providing such an analysis is doomed from the start. This leads him to abandon the idea of a "*general* theory of meaning" and to focus instead on theories of meaning for particular languages.

The next large section of Lecture I is devoted to an extended argument for the claim that a Tarskian truth theory for English can serve as the basis for a theory of meaning for English. Davidson begins with the idea that a semantic theory must be recursive, which he takes to be suggested by the productivity of human linguistic competence—the fact that there is no obvious upper bound on how many expressions we can produce or comprehend. He then notes that the problem of articulating a recursive theory of the truth of sentences in a first-order language is more tractable than the problem of articulating a recursive theory of meaning. If, as Davidson argues, a translational theory of meaning is also inadequate, the Tarskian alternative is, he believes, all that remains. Davidson identifies and highlights the similarities between his preferred Tarskian methodology and a Fregean theory of reference, but argues that the Fregean theory oversteps when it posits entities (functions) referred to by predicates and sentential connectives.

Lecture I concludes with the tantalizing suggestion that the logical forms associated with sentences by an empirically supported Tarskian truth theory for a language can be identified with the Chomskyan deep structures of those sentences.

Connections with Published Work

Lecture I includes quite a few ideas that Davidson did not discuss in any detail elsewhere, or about which he came to change his mind after 1970. For example, he distinguishes between metaphorical meaning and literal meaning, a distinction that he famously came to reject. And his brief arguments that linguistic meaning is irreducible and that a general theory of meaning is impossible are not repeated elsewhere. One wonders whether the absence of these arguments in Davidson's published work indicates that he later came to reject them, and, if so, for what reason.

The suggestion that the logical forms associated with sentences by a truth theory can be identified with Chomskyan deep structure had been discussed in Davidson's "Semantics for Natural Languages," which appeared in 1968. Davidson's discussion of the relationship between asserting, speaking the truth, convention, and games was eventually incorporated into "Communication and Convention," which appeared in 1984.

Lecture II: Truth and Ontology

One elegant feature of these collected lectures is Davidson's choice to juxtapose certain of them: that the lecture on truth should appear between the lecture on the theory of meaning and the lecture on the logical form of action sentences makes much more sense than their arrangement in Davidson's published collections, where the subject of adverbial modification is not treated in the volume on the philosophy of language. In point of fact, these three lectures (as well as the essays on which the latter two are based) belong together.

Lecture II begins with the thought that a Tarskian truth-theoretic semantics for a natural language can serve as a guide to ontology. This may seem surprising, Davidson suggests, since the T-sentences generated by such a semantics may at first blush seem to be truisms, and it would be surprising for a collection of truisms to serve as a guide to ontology. But a Tarskian truth-theoretic semantics is not merely a collection of T-sentences; it is a finitely axiomatized theory which entails a collection of T-sentences, and this is where, for Davidson, its ontological interest lies.

The thought that begins the lecture is then temporarily set aside, and Davidson embarks on a discussion of what sort of objects to identify as the primary bearers of truth and falsity. Davidson first argues that the truth of object-language sentences must be relativized to a speaker and a time: T-sentences should be of the form:

⌜S is true (in L) for s at t iff ϕ,⌝

where "S" is a constant denoting a sentence in the object language and "ϕ" is a variable ranging over sentences of the metalanguage.

Davidson then suggests that no further relativization is necessary, since any other candidate parameter for relativization, such as a demonstratum parameter, can be accounted for in terms of a speaker/time pair: the demonstratum associated with a given utterance produced by a speaker at a time is the object that that speaker is demonstrating at that time.

After briefly considering the idea that the primary bearers of truth are propositions or statements and rejecting it on the basis that positing propositions in addition to sentences is gratuitous, Davidson returns to the idea of a Tarskian truth-theoretic semantics as a guide to ontology. In light of the preceding discussion, he remarks that a Tarskian theory of truth requires at least an ontology containing sentences, individuals, and times. But what else might be required?

Here Davidson proceeds by comparing his preferred Tarskian theory with a number of competitors, including what he calls the "double-negation" theory of truth, according to which "is true" should be understood as a sentential operator with the same effect as double negation, and the idea that a sentence is true just in case it corresponds to a fact. He argues that the double-negation theory, while it is entirely ontologically noncommittal, fails to account for sentences in which truth is predicated of named propositions, such as "Fermat's last theorem is true." Similarly, he rejects a fact-based theory of truth on the basis that, given certain plausible assumptions, it can be shown that there is only one fact (the so-called "Great Fact argument"). This, Davidson suggests, deprives the fact-based theory of interest.

The final alternative Davidson considers is one that appeals to substitutional quantification. The substitutional approach to the semantics of quantified sentences interests Davidson because he believes that, if it were successful, it would show how to give an ontologically noncommittal semantics for those sentences. But, drawing on arguments originally due to John Wallace, Davidson argues that the substitutional account of quantification cannot be correct because it cannot account for the fact that (e.g.) if "Someone is wise" is true, then someone is wise.

Having finished his survey of alternative theories, Davidson sketches the Tarskian approach, focusing in particular on the notion of satisfaction of an open sentence by a sequence of entities. Since the Tarskian theory requires that we posit such sequences, it appears to require also that we posit the entities out of which they are constructed. Thus an adequate theory of natural language must, in the end, be ontologically committal: "Ontology comes in only with satisfaction, and satisfaction is an essential part of the machinery needed to run a recursive theory of truth that satisfies Convention T."

Connections with Published Work

Davidson's discussion in this lecture draws heavily on his "True to the Facts," which appeared in 1969. In particular, the discussions of the double-negation theory, the fact-based theory, and the comparison between the fact-based theory and Davidson's preferred satisfaction-based theory can be traced to the earlier paper, as can the argument that the truth of sentences need not be relativized to anything more than a speaker and a time. Davidson's argument about substitutional quantification, for which he thanks John Wallace, does not appear in "True to the Facts" or his later work, though he often cites Wallace's work on the subject, and he hints at a similar argument in "In Defense of Convention T" (1973).

Lecture III: Quotation

As Lecture III begins, Davidson signals that his attention has shifted from methodological remarks to the construction of semantic theories for particular natural language constructions. This project will occupy him for the next three lectures: the subject of Lecture III is quotation;

Lecture IV is devoted to ascriptions of attitude; and Lecture V concerns action sentences. In each case, Davidson proposes to examine extant theories to see if they satisfy Convention T, and, finding that they do not, proposes alternative analyses.

The first theory of quotation Davidson targets in his discussion is what he labels "the proper-name theory." According to the proper-name theory, an expression surrounded by quotation marks is a logically simple name which refers to the linguistic expression inside the quotes. This theory, he points out, has trouble accounting for cases in which quoted material is apparently both used and mentioned. But, more importantly, Davidson argues that if quoted expressions are unstructured names, then each one will have to be separately included in the lexicon of any language including a syntactic device for quotation. Given that any quoted expression can itself be quoted, this means that the lexicon for any such language will have infinite cardinality. Since Davidson holds for methodological reasons that an adequate semantic theory for a natural language must posit a finite lexicon, he takes this to be a decisive objection to the proper-name theory.

Since the problem with the proper-name theory was that it treated quoted expressions as unstructured, Davidson turns next to a theory that treats quotation marks as an operator which renders enclosed material self-referential. According to this "picture theory," quoted expressions are syntactically complex, consisting of the quoted material, on the one hand, and the quotation operator, on the other. The picture theory successfully evades the threat of a bloated lexicon; Davidson, however, rejects it on the basis that merely stipulating that quoted expressions are self-referential does not explain how quotation succeeds *by* picturing; stating the semantics for the operator does not require appeal to the picturing relation.

Davidson pauses at this point to consider the charge that operators like the picture-theoretic quotation mark and "believes that" (construed along Fregean lines) are deviant in that the meanings of expressions, when they occur within the scope of such operators, are not functions of their meanings in other linguistic contexts. He suggests that this feature of the picture theory of quotation is in principle avoidable; one can treat all words as referring, by default, to themselves, and treat the absence of quotation as an operator which restores to expressions their intuitive referents.

The last theory Davidson considers before presenting his own is one that combines elements of the previous two. According to this "spelling theory," a quoted simple expression (a letter or other individual typographical element) refers to itself, as on the proper-name theory; however, a quoted complex expression abbreviates the definite description that describes the sequence of simple expressions which, when concatenated, form it. Like the picture theory, the spelling theory avoids the problem of an infinitary lexicon. Davidson, however, objects that quotation marks play no essential role in the spelling theory, and that it predicts that one should be able to quantify into the quotation operator. He also argues that the spelling theory cannot account for our ability to introduce novel notation, such as Greek letters, using quotation.

Having found all competing theories unsatisfactory, Davidson concludes by describing his own proposal, the so-called "demonstrative theory." According to the demonstrative theory, quotation marks refer to the material they flank, which is not always a semantic part of the sentence containing it. The flexibility of demonstrative reference, Davidson claims, allows his theory to account for mixed use/mention cases: in these cases, the demonstrative introduced by the quotation marks refers to a part of the sentence that does make a semantic contribution. Moreover, since the demonstrative theory reduces quotation to demonstration, it is susceptible to a truth-theoretic treatment if demonstratives are. Since Davidson takes the semantics of demonstratives to require no more than the relativization of truth conditions to speakers and times, he takes the demonstrative theory to succeed in meeting the constraints imposed by Convention T.

Connections with Published Work

The text of Lecture III is similar to the text of Davidson's "Quotation," which appeared nine years later. The lecture thus demonstrates that Davidson's account of quotation was developed much earlier than is apparent from his history of publications. The most significant difference between Lecture III and the published version of "Quotation" is that the latter does not include Davidson's discussion of the "reverse" picture theory, according to which all expressions refer to themselves by default and reference to the nonlinguistic world is induced by a covert non-quotation operator.

In the text of the lecture, Davidson claims that this "reverse" theory avoids positing an operator that violates compositionality by interacting with material in its scope in a way that cannot be predicted on the basis of the semantic properties of that material. The idea seems to be that, while the ordinary picture theory requires the quotation operator to operate on (e.g.) "dog" and "hound," which have the same semantic properties, and produce different results, the reverse theory assigns "dog" and "hound" (and indeed any two distinct words) different semantic properties, thus preserving compositionality.

The reverse picture theory is subject to a number of difficulties. For example, it struggles to account for lexical ambiguity: all of the lexical items in the sentence "Jones went to the bank," for example, are unambiguous, referring as they do to themselves. It follows that if the non-quotation operator is not to violate compositionality, it must either map "bank" to the property of being a financial institution in all linguistic contexts or map it to the property of being the side of a river in all linguistic contexts. Either way, one reading of "Jones went to the bank" will be lost. Given that Davidson does not ultimately endorse the reverse picture theory, however, it remains unclear why he eliminated discussion of it from the published version of "Quotation."

Lecture IV: Attributions of Attitude

The subject of Lecture IV is attributions of attitude. In it, Davidson extends his theory of indirect quotation ("On Saying That," 1968) to propositional attitudes generally, where these are individuated syntactically as verbs that can take a sentence or "that"-clause as internal argument. Before introducing the main subject of the paper, however, Davidson reflects on some methodological issues raised by his discussion of quotation in the previous lecture. The dialectic surrounding quotation, he argues, has a familiar form: first, the observation that a traditional theory is inadequate; second, an attempt to solve the problem syncategorematically; third, the realization that this syncategorematic solution requires an infinite lexicon and is, therefore, untenable. Davidson's remarks here constitute a refreshing and atypically unhedged meta-discussion of how philosophy progresses.

In the case of quotation, we have seen that Davidson argues that the proper-name theory, which treats quoted expressions as semantically primitive, is unacceptable because it requires positing an infinitary lexicon. Davidson now claims that this kind of syncategorematic treatment is in fact desirable when it does not lead to unacceptable consequences, since it allows us to make our semantic theory for a given object language less ontologically committal. Opting for syncategorematic analyses whenever possible allows us to discover which entities we are forced to posit in order to account for human linguistic practice.

Having made this methodological point, Davidson turns to the problem of constructing a truth theory for attributions of attitude. After distinguishing his subject from the problem of constructing a reductive analysis of belief, he settles on "asserted that" sentences as the primary focus of his theoretical attention. Davidson argues that the dialectic surrounding attributions of attitude parallels the dialectic surrounding quotation in that, once it was realized that expressions inside attitude ascriptions do not behave semantically as they do outside, theoreticians opted for syncategorematic treatments. Here he mentions Quine, to whom he attributes the view that every combination of an attitude verb and a complement clause is a distinct semantically unstructured predicate of speakers, and Scheffler, who defends a view which is similar except that the predicates are taken to be predicates of utterances, as well as theories that treat the complement clauses of attitude ascriptions as complex adverbial modifiers.

More controversially, Davidson argues that the theories of Church and Frege are subject to the same problem as those of Quine and Scheffler. For Davidson, Church's theory, which involves introducing subscripts for lexical items that appear in ascriptions of attitude, amounts to positing an infinite number of homonymous expressions corresponding to each natural language word. Frege's theory, which instead makes the interpretation of lexical items in ascriptions of attitude depend on the number of attitude verbs under which they are embedded, does not introduce an infinity of lexical items; nevertheless, it illicitly "welds" together "an expression plus an index gotten by counting the number of occurrences of verbs of attitude that dominate it."

It is not impossible to produce a truth-theoretically tractable theory of attitude ascriptions by appealing to intensions, however. If a theory that appeals only to extensions and intensions is viable (for example, if expressions behave in the same way whether they are singly or multiply embedded under attitude verbs), then one could have expressions refer primarily to their intensions, introducing an operator that would apply to them to make them refer to their extensions. Davidson concedes that such a theory would be viable; he argues that it would not be satisfactory, however, for at least two reasons. First, he argues that positing intensions in order to solve the problem of attitude reports is a bad-making feature of a semantic theory—it would be preferable to get by without any entities introduced for purely theoretical reasons. Second, he argues that the complementizer clauses in ascriptions of attitude cannot name intensions or propositions because the propositional attitude ascribed by any particular attitude ascription is not fixed by the conventions of language, being instead dependent on myriad contextual factors.

Where have the theories Davidson has canvassed so far gone wrong? His suggestion is that they have regarded the syntactically embedded sentence, which characterizes the attitude ascribed, as *semantically* a part of the embedding sentence. Much better, Davidson argues, to regard attitude ascriptions along the lines of *discourses*, in which utterances are first made and then referred to using demonstratives, as in "The moon constitutes a severe threat to our security. This was asserted yesterday by the Mayor of the Indian Ocean." In such discourses, there is no temptation to regard the demonstrative "this" in the second sentence as somehow forcing the expressions in the first to have anything other than their normal semantic values. But if it is possible to produce and then refer to an utterance in this way, there is no in-principle reason why sincerely uttering one sentence, syntactically considered, might not involve doing both. This is, in fact, what Davidson suggests: according to his "paratactic analysis" of attitude ascriptions, they involve demonstrative reference to an utterance of the speaker's, which is claimed to stand in some relation to some utterance or attitude of the ascribee. Thus, the sentence "Heraclitus said that everything flows" is analyzed as "Some act of saying performed by Heraclitus was synonymous with the following act of saying (performed by me): Everything flows"; similarly, the sentence "Thales believed that there is a god in the magnet" is analyzed as "Some belief of Thales had the content expressed by the following act of saying (performed by me): There is a god in the magnet."

Davidson turns next to the question of first-person attributions of attitude. How is it, he wonders, that claiming that someone else asserts that the earth moves does not involve asserting oneself that the earth moves, but claiming that one asserts that the earth moves does sometimes involve asserting oneself that the earth moves? More generally, how is it that these first-person attitude ascriptions manage to perform the speech acts they report? Davidson regards it as a virtue of his theory that it can account for such performative uses of first-personal ascriptions of attitude. His suggestion is that, in performative cases, a single pronounced sentence both constitutes the performance of a speech act and serves to characterize the content of that speech act. Thus the sentence "I assert that the earth moves" is analyzed as "My next remark is synonymous with a present assertion of mine: The earth moves."

Davidson concludes with a discussion of the relationship between clausal mood and what he calls "mode" (illocutionary force). He points out that mood is a matter of linguistic meaning, whereas mode is not, arguing that this observation undermines attempts to demonstrate that imperatives and interrogatives are non-truth-conditional. He then proposes a truth-conditional account of imperative clausal mood which parallels his paratactic analysis of indicative performatives like "assert." According to Davidson's proposal, imperative clauses are underlyingly quite complex, so that the sentence "Close the door," for example, is interpreted as "The next remark is imperative in mode. You will close the door."

Connections with Published Work

Lecture IV draws on the paratactic account of indirect speech reports developed in "On Saying That" (1968), though it significantly generalizes that account by extending it to all forms of propositional attitude ascriptions—a strategy that Davidson mentions briefly in his 1976 "Reply to Foster." Although "On Saying That" does include a condensed version of Davidson's objections to the theories of attitude ascriptions proposed by Frege and Church, Lecture IV provides a lengthier exposition, and in this sense prefigures the discussion that would later appear in "The Method of Truth in Metaphysics" (1977). Davidson's discussion of mood and mode at the end of Lecture IV is clearly the predecessor of his much later essay "Moods and Performances" (1979).

Lecture V: Adverbial Modification

At the beginning of Lecture V, Davidson briefly pauses his project of analyzing troublesome constructions in natural language to offer a number of methodological remarks. Modifying Convention T allows us to account for indexicality in natural language, and Davidson has labored in the previous lectures to show that once we are able to accommodate demonstrative reference within a Tarskian theory, we can also accommodate quotation and attributions of attitude. Davidson now argues that the Tarskian approach he has been advocating—which can account for the logic of truth-conditional connectives, quantifiers, indexicals, quotation, attitude ascriptions, mood, and performatives—should also be able to accommodate descriptions, and might be able to accommodate non-referring singular terms and truth-value gaps. In fact, Davidson describes three reasons for holding that a Tarskian approach will ultimately be able to accommodate the full range of natural language constructions. (This is a clear departure from the skepticism at the end of "Truth and Meaning" with regard to an exhaustive treatment of natural language, based on Tarskian considerations.)

The first of Davidson's reasons is that the Tarskian project may, in fact, be more flexible than is commonly recognized: the logic on which a T-theory is based need not be standard first-order logic, as long as it is possible to construct a theory of truth for it. His second reason is that work in generative syntax has brought work in linguistics much closer to work in logic in at least two respects: first, in particular choices like the choice to treat pronouns as variables and the choice to assign common nouns, (intransitive) verbs, and adjectives meanings of the same semantic type; second, in its general willingness to posit underlying levels of representation which differ radically from the prima facie structure of natural language phrases. Davidson's third reason has the flavor of a transcendental deduction: it is a condition for the possibility of our linguistic competence in assigning truth conditions to arbitrary sentences, he argues, that there exists some finite recursive theory for our language satisfying Convention T.

Having outlined his reasons for optimism about the Tarskian program, Davidson returns to the project of analyzing particular constructions—in this case, adverbial modifiers. Presumably because his analysis of adverbial modifiers will ultimately rely heavily on an ontology of events, he begins by discussing whether the semanticist is committed to such entities even before considering adverbs. A simple argument for adding events to one's semantic metalanguage is that sentences like "The chairman's resignation preceded the fall of the government" appear to contain singular terms which refer to events. Davidson considers and rejects a strategy for resisting this argument by assimilating the semantics of "The chairman's resignation preceded the fall of the government" to that of "The chairman resigned before the government fell." He has two arguments against this alternative, apparently event-free proposal: first, that "the chairman's resignation" either entails or presupposes the uniqueness of the resignation event, so that the two sentences, in fact, have different truth conditions; second, that a proper treatment of "before" will require the introduction of quantification over times, and a proper treatment of causal and explanatory connectives ("caused," "because," etc.) will similarly require the introduction of quantification over events. So the strategy ultimately fails to escape the necessity of positing events.

If, moreover, one adopts the methodology of assigning the same semantic contribution to sentences when they appear freestanding as when they appear embedded under connectives, then the realization that sentences embedded in causal and explanatory claims quantify over events requires that we hold that they also do so when they appear unembedded. Davidson's conception of natural language thus involves a pervasive covert substructure of quantification over events.

Davidson turns next to adverbial modification, presenting his semantic treatment of adverbs as a further argument for the claim that natural language sentences covertly quantify over events. He begins by noting the "variable polyadicity" of adverbial phrases, which is constituted by their syntactic and semantic capacity to accept a seemingly arbitrary number of modifiers—of time, location, manner, duration, and so forth. A naive logical treatment of verbs of action assigns them predicates or relations with fixed adicities (generally between one and three)—thus "smiled" is assigned a predicate, and "kicked" is assigned a binary relation. The diversity and optionality of adverbial modifiers seems, however, to doom such an approach: we are forced to represent each natural language verb with an indefinitely large set of relations of different adicities corresponding to the indefinitely large set of combinations of adverbial modifiers with which it could co-occur.

Davidson's solution to this problem is to treat verbs of action and change as introducing quantification over events, and to treat adverbial modifiers as introducing descriptive material into the scope of the event quantifier. This solves the problem of variable polyadicity by rendering the process of adverbial modification both compositional and recursive. The translation of natural language sentences into event descriptions, however, is not always straightforward; for example, in order to accommodate the ambiguity in the sentence "John broke the window," we need to posit a complex underlying representation containing two events: one the breaking of the window and the other some sort of movement. On one reading (the one where John breaks the window using some unspecified object), the movement in question will be one intentionally produced by John; on the other reading (the one where John jumps or is flung though the window), the movement will be one of John himself. Nevertheless, the main target for analysis— modification by adjunction—is given a very natural treatment, where (for example), the meaning of the preposition "at," on its temporal interpretation, is such that it combines with an expression denoting a time to form a predicate of events. Thus, the sentence "John smiled at eleven o'clock" is interpreted as "There was a smiling event of which John was the agent and which occurred at eleven o'clock."

By way of concluding his discussion of adverbial modification, Davidson offers two caveats. First, the account does not extend naturally to adverbs like "intentionally," which induce linguistics environments in which the substitution of coreferential expressions fails to preserve truth; Davidson suggests that sentences containing such adverbs be analyzed along the lines of his account of ascriptions of attitude. Second, adverbs like "well" and "quickly" resist assimilation to Davidson's semantic framework, since events seem to be individuated too coarsely to be described as *good* or *fast*. To use Davidson's example, a single event could be both a good dancing and a poor seduction of the king. Davidson does not offer any proposed solution to this problem, merely noting it as a difficulty and moving on.

Having presented his analysis of adverbial modification, Davidson turns back to methodological remarks in the last third of the lecture. First, he notes that, now that a concrete proposal about the semantics of adverbial modification is on the table, we can assess various adverbial strategies for doing away with apparent ontological commitments. Since Davidson's proposal introduces an extensive ontology of events, it is not nominalistic in spirit; this, he expects, will disappoint advocates of most adverbial strategies. Second, he embarks on an extensive discussion of the notion of logical form.

A sentence, Davidson argues, should not be thought to have a unique logical form. Instead, the claim that an object-language sentence has a particular logical form must be relativized to both an underlying logical metalanguage (complete with a definition of entailment) and a method for translating object-language sentences into this metalanguage. Davidson's proposals about the logical forms of various English sentences should be interpreted, he maintains, as claims that the particular choices of a logical metalanguage and a translation procedure that he favors are particularly good ones.

To exhibit the advantages of his choices of logical form, Davidson contrasts them with the logical forms posited by an imagined theory which (as we have seen before) assigns to each natural language verb of action an indefinitely large set of logical relations of different adicity, but somehow manages to introduce rules of inference which preserve the intuitive entailment relations between, for example, the sentence "The ball rolled to the bush" and the sentence "The ball rolled." Davidson lists a number of virtues of his proposal as compared to this imagined one: its logic is known to be consistent and complete with respect to standard model theory; it posits fewer inference rules; and it follows intuition in treating "rolled" as univocal—as contributing a "common conceptual element" to the interpretation of every sentence in which it occurs.

Connections with Published Work

Lecture V draws heavily on Davidson's essay "The Logical Form of Action Sentences," which had appeared three years earlier in 1967. However, Lecture V differs from that earlier work in that it integrates discussion of a number of points that emerged in Davidson's exchanges with various commentators between 1966 and 1970. For example, the discussion of the sentence "the chairman's resignation preceded the fall of the government," the analogy to Frege's theory of tense, the remarks on logical form, and the argument against appealing to additional inference rules all draw on Davidson's reply to James Cargile, published in 1970 (the analogy to Frege also reappears later in Davidson's 1977 "The Method of Truth in Metaphysics"). The discussion of the sentence "the rock broke the window" appears to have been inspired by Davidson's exchange with Héctor-Neri Castañeda, published in 1967. The methodological remarks in the first few pages of Lecture V appear to have been newly written for Davidson's Oxford audience.

It would also be remiss not to mention that this lecture comfortably and correctly situates Davidson's discussion of adverbial modification (and action and event sentences) within his program in the philosophy of language. When "The Logical Form of Action Sentences" was collected in 1980, Davidson included it with his work in action theory rather than philosophy of language, even though it is a paradigmatic discussion in, and perhaps his most lasting and appreciated contribution to, semantics.

Lecture VI: Invariants of Translation

In Lecture VI, Davidson turns away from the project of providing analyses for particular natural language constructions, which has occupied him for the previous three lectures, and back to questions of methodology. The issue he addresses in this final lecture is an epistemic one: how can we come to know that a candidate T-theory for an object language is correct? Davidson, following Quine, refers to this as the problem of *radical translation*. In the general case—the case where it is not assumed that the theoretician has any antecedent knowledge of the object language—there will be no theory-independent way of knowing whether the T-sentences derivable in the theory are translational. One must therefore look for a criterion of success for a T-theory that does not presuppose that its T-sentences are translational. It is interesting to note that Davidson does not take pains in this lecture—as he does in his published work—to distance himself from Quine both in terms of methodology and by labeling his approach "radical interpretation" rather than "radical translation."

A T-theory attempts to pair object-language sentences with the conditions under which one who speaks them speaks the truth, in the sense of speaking the truth Davidson articulates in Lecture I. Since Davidson's notion of speaking the truth is independent of speakers' intentions, it fits naturally into a theory designed to capture the purely linguistic rules governing the verbal behavior of a speech community (as opposed, for example, to a theory of the speech acts performed by members of the community). To describe a linguistic performance as a speaking of the truth (or as a failing to do so), Davidson reminds us, is not to characterize the non-linguistic goals (roughly, the perlocutionary intentions) of its author; neither is it to characterize what in Austinian terminology would be called the illocutionary act performed, since a given illocutionary act can be performed by uttering any number of different sentences; it is, instead, to characterize the locutionary act performed (the action described "in terms of [the speaker's] actual words and the intentions necessary to uttering a particular sentence with shared truth conditions as an act of communication."

An obvious way to test a Tarskian truth theory for an arbitrary object language would be to assess whether it could be used to prove some representative T-sentences for the object language. Unfortunately, since part of what it is to be a T-sentence is for the material that comes on the right-hand side of the biconditional to be a translation of the object-language sentence described on the left-hand side, there is no theory-independent way to know which sentences are T-sentences.

Davidson suggests that (i) we will be able to identify the genuine T-sentences if we are able to identify which sentences with the form of T-sentences are true, and (ii) it is possible to identify which sentences with the form of T-sentences are true. This latter possibility claim is predicated on two methodological assumptions. First, Davidson assumes that we will not be led too far astray if we assume that whenever an object-language speaker accepts a sentence, that sentence is true. Second, Davidson assumes that we, as theoreticians, are correct about which propositions that are candidate meanings for object-language sentences are true. Granting these two assumptions, we are entitled, on the basis of observing that our subject accepts the sentence "Baarish ho rahii hai" when it is raining in his vicinity, to conclude that the sentence "Baarish ho rahii hai" is true in the subject's language iff it is raining. Davidson says little about how the theoretician is to determine whether her subject accepts a given sentence rather than bearing some other doxastic attitude toward it; he assumes that behavioral cues will render this epistemic problem tractable.

The project of pairing accepted sentences with true propositions is still fairly unconstrained, and Davidson suggests that the crucial factor in making it tractable is that the pairing must be effected in such a way that the underlying recursive structure of the object language is revealed. Since the recursive structures with which we are antecedently familiar are those of our own language, we will tend to find these in the object language, as well. In the context of Davidson's prior arguments, this amounts to the claim that the recursive structure we will uncover in the process of radical translation is first-order quantificational structure. The idea that first-order quantificational theory underlies all languages is, for Davidson, an empirical hypothesis; the idea that some single recursive theory (whatever that might be) underlies all languages is not, being instead a condition for the possibility of translation between them.

Davidson now turns to a skeptical worry: given his methodological assumptions, the theorist will never attribute massive, systematic error to the speakers of an object language—how could she, given that in choosing which propositions to pair with which accepted sentences, she assumes that speakers only accept sentences which express true propositions? But doesn't this conclusion rule out by fiat a genuine possibility, which is that the speakers of some language really do make massive, systematic errors about the facts? Davidson claims that this is not a genuine but improbable possibility; a theory that attributes such massive, systematic error to speakers of the object language is *unintelligible*. To endorse a theory that attributes such error is to undermine one's evidence for endorsing the theory.

This point about the limits of error applies not only in the context of radical translation, Davidson proceeds to argue; it also applies to our own beliefs. Davidson's argument for this radical conclusion is as follows: a person trying to interpret the language and beliefs of an omniscient informant would necessarily construct a theory according to which most of his or her own beliefs are true, as well.

The inevitability of discovering the recursive structure of our own language in the languages of others, as well as the preponderance of our beliefs in the minds of our peers, leads Davidson to reconceive of the project of semantics as an inquiry into the structural features of reality. For if there is a single recursive structure underlying all languages, then the ontological commitments of that structure are the ontological commitments of language in general. It is here that Davidson introduces the notion of an *invariant of translation*, a sentence the truth of which is preserved when switching between theories of a given phenomenon. If today's temperature is greater than yesterday's temperature as measured in degrees Fahrenheit, for example, then it is greater than yesterday's temperature as measured on any scale. Thus, sentences about the ordering of days induced by temperature measurement are invariant under translation between different theories of temperature. Similarly, Davidson suggests, there might be claims that are invariant under translation between adequate truth theories for a given language. While some claims about the existence of particular entities are unlikely to be invariants of translation, general commitments to classes of entities like events, which are imposed by the structure of quantificational theory, are more plausible candidates.

Davidson concludes by distinguishing his preferred approach to the study of language from those that begin by assigning meanings to particular expressions. The concept of a meaning, he claims, presupposes a semantic theory. There is thus no genuine alternative to his holistic methodology—interpretive hypotheses are not justified piecemeal, but rather by "the whole fabric of belief as evinced in a system of behavior."

Connections with Published Work

Davidson's approach to radical translation appears in its first published form in "Radical Interpretation" (1973) though it is prefigured by some brief remarks in "Truth and Meaning" (1967). It is worth noting that in "Radical Interpretation," Davidson places much more emphasis on the methodological differences between his approach and Quine's (hence the title's reference to radical *interpretation* rather than radical *translation*). Lecture VI may thus represent an earlier period in his thought, during which the differences between his own approach and Quine's seemed less significant. His "omniscient informant" argument seems to be a predecessor of the "omniscient interpreter" argument, which was first presented in "The Method of Truth in Metaphysics" (1977). Davidson in *Inquiries into Truth and Interpretation* (1984) remarks that "On the Very Idea of a Conceptual Scheme" (1974) is the direct descendant of Lecture VI.

Lecture I
Speaking the Truth (May 13, 1970)

When someone speaks the truth, speaker, language, and the world come into a relation that is worthy of, and amenable to, systematic study. Not that this is entirely obvious. Speaking the truth is not our most common or most important linguistic activity. So it needs showing if, as I think, a theory of the conditions under which someone speaks the truth may serve as the foundation of a theory of meaning.

Let me focus attention on an aspect of speaking the truth that sets it apart from much of the rest of linguistic behavior, and helps explain its central role in theory. What helps to distinguish speaking the truth is this: the question whether someone has done it on a particular occasion is wholly determined by systematic facts about the language that must be known to anyone who speaks or understands the language. Of course, this doesn't mean that anyone who knows the language always knows when a speaker has spoken the truth. Rather, what he knows, together with the way the world is, determines whether the truth was spoken. Thus someone who knows English knows that: an utterance of the sentence "Snow is white" is an occasion when the truth is spoken if and only if snow is white. And this fact, together with the way the world is, determines whether someone who utters the sentence "Snow is white" speaks the truth.

I labor this simple relation between the knowledge a speaker of a language has and speaking the truth because it is so nearly unique. It is hard to think of a single further and interesting case of a linguistic action which is such that, simply by knowing the language, one can state a criterion determining whether that action has been performed. Asserting, ordering, insulting, promising, describing, warning, instructing, questioning, and stating are actions that can be performed by those who have the gift of speech, but in not one of these cases, I think, can knowledge of the criteria that determine whether one of these actions has been performed be called exclusively linguistic knowledge.

Take assertion as the example. We know how to make assertions, and we can tell, usually, when an assertion has been made; and if the language is

The Structure of Truth: The 1970 John Locke Lectures. Cameron Domenico Kirk-Giannini and Ernie Lepore,
Oxford University Press (2020). © Cameron Domenico Kirk-Giannini and Ernie Lepore.
DOI: 10.1093/oso/9780198842491.001.0001

ours, *what* has been asserted. But what is it we know? Let someone speak the sentence "Snow is white"; I know what determines whether he speaks the truth; but what determines whether he has made an assertion? In the context of speech there are normally all the clues that are needed to decide whether an assertion has been made. But there is no *rule* for telling, because there is no rule or procedure by following which a speaker can be sure of making an assertion. Making an assertion, like performing most other linguistic actions, is unlike speaking the truth: our knowledge of how to do it, and how to recognize that it has been done, includes, but transcends, our systematic knowledge of the language.

Suppose, contrary to fact, that there were a conventional device that represented the speaker as making an assertion: let us say, the speaker prefaces an utterance with the words "I hereby assert that"; he says this in a deep and sonorous tone of voice, and crosses his heart as he speaks. Now that we know the device, however, what on earth can prevent some clown from putting on the assertion-skit as a joke, as nothing but a skit? In which case we no longer have an assertion. It is no help to add that part of what is required is that the speaker must be *sincere*. That's just the point; sincerity can't be part of a convention. Convention is a substitute for sincerity, but cannot depend on it.

What encourages the illusion that there are rules for making assertions, promising, commanding, and the like, is that there *are* rules for finding sentences such that if they are uttered with certain intentions in typical or standard situations, then their being uttered constitutes the making of an assertion or a promise, or the issuing of a command. But unless we can reduce to the form of a rule of language the features of a situation that make it typical or standard (including the relevant intentions), we will not have eliminated the contrast I am drawing between speaking the truth on the one hand and asserting, promising, and commanding on the other.

Speaking the truth is like winning in games such as chess or bridge in that it can be done only by performing within the norms and conventions that constitute the activity: a definition of what it is to win is part of the definition of the game of chess, or of contract bridge; a definition of what it is to speak the truth is (at least) part of the definition of a language. But in two important respects, speaking the truth is quite unlike winning at a game. First, there is no presumption that someone who speaks wants or intends to speak the truth, or, if he does speak the truth, that he does it intentionally. The parallel presumptions do hold in the case of winning. And, second, speaking the truth is very seldom, or perhaps never, an end in itself, while it is essential to the character of a game that winning can be, and typically is, an end in itself.

Making an assertion is more like playing a game in which winning is possible, for someone who makes an assertion represents himself in a certain light; he represents himself as believing what he says, much as the player represents himself as wanting (or intending to try) to win. In each case the representation may be deceitful. Or it may not, even when the speaker or player is not what he represents himself to be. Someone playing chess may not intend to deceive his partner into thinking he wants to win; this does not conflict with the sense in which he must, if he plays at all, represent himself as aiming to win. Somewhat analogously, someone who makes an assertion represents himself as believing what he says, even though he may not, in making his assertion, intend to cause his hearer to believe that he believes what he says, or intend to cause his hearer to believe that he intends to cause his hearer to believe what he says.

Making an assertion is, then, like playing a game in a respect in which speaking the truth is not—there is at least the symbolic evocation of a purpose guiding the activity. But the difference remains that this purpose, whether real or merely represented, can, in the case of a game, but not in the case of language, be wholly defined in terms of conventional procedures.

In brief, the following feature characterizes (and might even be said to define) a large class of games: there is an end (winning) that players often do have, and that any player must represent himself as having; this end can be achieved only by engaging in activities explicitly given by rules, and how the end is achieved is defined by the rules. As far as I can see, *no* linguistic behavior has this feature i.e. a feature analogous to winning in a game.

Asserting, commanding, promising, and questioning are not good subjects of investigation if we want to study what is peculiarly linguistic, because in performing such actions we necessarily operate beyond the reach of the conventions of language. Speaking the truth, on the other hand, is specially suited to systematic study just because the conditions for speaking the truth are a matter of linguistic convention. What explains this possibility in part is that speaking the truth is essentially disengaged: it is not done for its own sake, nor, typically, for the sake of any other end; we often do not know it has been done, and do not care. (Perhaps it is obvious on reflection that systematic theory of meaning must be based on a feature of speech behavior that is disengaged in this way.)

Up to this point I have been trying to ignore the plain fact that the expression "Speaking the truth" is by no means unambiguous, and only one of its meanings is appropriate to these remarks and claims. In fact, without gloss the phrase will not take the weight I have been putting on it.

If someone utters the sentence "Socrates was married to Xanthippe," does he speak the truth? Let the answer depend just on whether Socrates was married to Xanthippe, and the phrase "speak the truth" has been used in the way I want. Obviously there are other ways of using it. To say someone didn't speak the truth often implies a rebuke, and when it does, something of the idea of assertion seems to have crept into the idea of speaking—just what it takes to spoil the purity that made me favor the notion of speaking the truth in the first place.

We might persuade ourselves to set aside some of these potentially worrisome cases, but there is no lightly disposing of the non-literal cases. I have in mind examples such as these: I say of a man whose strength amazes me, "He can lift a ton"; of a woman who nags, "She's a witch"; I say to my waiting friend, "I'll be there in a second." But I know, and I know my hearers know, that the strong man *cannot* lift a ton, that there are no witches, that it will be more than a second before I get there. Do I fail to speak the truth?

These examples, or better ones, invite us to distinguish between occasions on which what a speaker says is true if and only if his *words* are true (or express a truth) and those occasions on which the truth of what *he says* may differ from the truth of what his words express. Is this a distinction that can be made sharp without begging the interesting questions?

It will not help, or certainly not much, to say that in one case the speaker says what he means and in the other not. For there is no clear sense in which, in the imagined cases, I fail to say what I mean. A man who does not say what he means either does it on purpose, in which case he is being devious, or he does it inadvertently, in which case he fails in some way in what he intended. But the examples do not hint of the devious, nor of relevant failure.

We are on the wrong track. Cases where we do, and cases where we do not, say what we mean are mutually exclusive, while cases where our words mean one thing and we another are not. The point is even plainer if put in terms of truth instead of meaning: the obvious falsity of his words may often be an intended signal that a speaker does not mean what his words do; this may even aid him in saying something true. Irony, exaggeration, metonymy, and metaphor provide conspicuous illustrations. If a child is eating peas with a knife his father may say sternly, "No one eats peas with a knife in this house." The father's words depend, for their effect, on the hearer recognizing them as false; yet though we would not call the father's remonstration true, it is not false either.

The awkward phrases "The words are true," "What the words mean," may suggest that this kind of truth and meaning, the kind we attribute to the words, is not tied to or relative to a speaker and a time, thus differing from what is said. The suggestion is false. The truth of the words "Socrates was married to Xanthippe" depends on *when* they are spoken, just as the truth of what is said by someone who utters them does.

The meaning of a sentence is less relative to circumstances of utterance than truth; indeed, one way to conceive the meaning of a sentence is as a function that maps a speaker and a time (and perhaps other features of the environment) onto a truth value. Still, this function will be different for different speakers of the same sentence, so relativity is reinstated, though perhaps at a different level.

These remarks are meant to dampen the optimism of anyone inclined to think not only that we call attention to a distinction with the phrases "what the speaker means" and "what the words mean" but also that in appealing to the phrases we take a step toward clarifying the distinction. A step would have been taken if words or sentences had meanings that depended not at all on occasion of use; but this is not the case.

Degree of abstraction is nevertheless to the point. No person has a heart as big as a whale, which is why, when Johnny says, "Frankie had a heart as big as a whale," there is a clear sense in which what he says is false. But if Frankie was kind and generous to a fault, there is another sense in which Johnny spoke the truth. Someone might know that (in this sense) Johnny spoke the truth when he said "Frankie had a heart as big as a whale" without knowing what the words mean, much less that they express an obvious falsehood. Nevertheless, any fact that is relevant to establishing that, in one sense, Johnny said something false, is relevant to establishing that, in the other sense, he said something true. What makes the saying literally false, namely the large size of the heart of a whale, is part of what it takes to make it figuratively true. A hearer would not understand Johnny's statement in the sense in which it is true unless he knew its truth conditions in the sense in which they, and the world, make it false.

An analogous point can be made about the speaker and his intentions. Johnny intends, in saying "Frankie had a heart as big as a whale," to say something true; he also intends to utter words that are false. The second intention nests inside the first: he intends to say something true by uttering a sentence which is true if and only if Frankie had a heart as big as a whale—a sentence that is therefore false.

*   *   *

As a prolegomenon to the systematic study of linguistic meaning, I have been striving to isolate a *conventional semantic core* of acts of speech, a core that determines at least the literal truth of sentences as spoken. In the attempt to single out the sort of meaning and truth upon which communication by language depends, I have not hesitated to use such concepts as that of the literal truth of an utterance, the meaning (of a sentence), a rule of usage, or a convention of language. So even if it were now quite clear (which of course it is not) exactly what constitutes the conventional semantic core, we could hardly advertise this as progress towards an analysis of meaning, since we have uncritically used the concepts it is our project to illuminate.

The courageous course would be to start again and see whether, by moving much more slowly and carefully, we could abstract conventional linguistic meaning from the nexus of behavior in which it is conceptually embedded without drawing, directly or indirectly, on the notions to be abstracted. Real ambition might try to get along without using any mental concepts, such as belief, meaning (in the non-linguistic sense), or intention, giving as a reason for such abstemiousness the ground (by no means absurd) that all such concepts necessarily draw on semantic resources. A more modest range of strategies would allow appeal to notions like intending, say, and belief, but not that of a rule or convention, or at least not that of a *linguistic* convention.

I cannot share these brave dreams of giving a radical explanation of linguistic meaning in terms of something simpler, or different. The attempts, by empiricists and others, to analyze what goes on when we use language in terms of stimulus and response, of avoidance behavior, of patterns of sensory stimulations, substitute goal-objects, or intentions that others should respond to our expressed intentions, seem to me misguided from the start. What they set out to do cannot, I think, be done. Philosophers have thought it could for the reason that has provoked so many forms of reduction: the belief (false, but infinitely tempting) that because all our evidence for what a man means can be stated in a vocabulary as brutally free from the intensional as one pleases, it *must* be possible to reduce truths about meaning to truths about the non-intensional. Even supposing the premises of this bit of reasoning to be clear and true, the conclusion does not follow in any interesting sense. We seem to have to learn this anew for almost every branch of philosophy and every decade. Most of us know that intensional concepts can't be reduced to extensional but have yet to acknowledge that meaning, in its strictly linguistic sense (intension with an "s"), can't be reduced to the notion of intention (intention with a "t").

Although I shan't attempt to show it now, the irreducibility of linguistic meaning seems to me to be susceptible of something like proof. The reason is that although what we say depends, among other things, on what our *words* mean, the dependency the other way can't be formulated without begging the question. The reason is, as I suggested before, the autonomy of the conventional in the context of an overriding (i.e. non-linguistic) intention. It is no help to appeal to such concepts as those of what is typically, usually, honestly, or sincerely intended, nor to ring in a distinction between "central" and "parasitic" uses of language. In spelling out the exact nature of the sincerity involved, or what it is precisely that must be honestly intended, or in locating the central uses, a forbidden concept will be needed.

How do we go on? We must, in the first place, abandon the idea of a *general* theory of meaning, i.e. a serious theory applying to languages in general. This seems inevitable anyway, for the following reason. Any competent theory of meaning must include or entail a theory of truth. But then a general theory of meaning would include a general theory of truth, and this we know there cannot be, on pain of contradiction. Relativizing truth to speakers and times, or thinking of it as an attribute of statements, utterances, or "things said," rather than sentences, does not, contrary to what is often claimed, lead to any simple solution of the semantic paradoxes.

What can be reasonably attempted is a constructive account of linguistic (literal) meaning for a particular language. Such an account must, if I am right, accept as unreduced the concept of the utterance of a sentence by a speaker as a linguistic act. The contribution of theory will then consist entirely in its providing a systematic description of the semantic structure of the totality of such acts, potential and real. The distinction between literal meaning and something broader, the distinction we have been discussing between what a speaker means and what his words mean, cannot be *used* (except as an informal guide) in constructing the theory; but we can, if we please, say that the semantic core of a particular language *is* what the theory describes.

The fact that a theory of meaning must be a theory for a particular language (by which I mean only, a theory for a class of speakers) does not imply that such a theory has no bearing on other languages. On the contrary, if a theory of the kind I think we can reasonably try to devise were available for one language, it would be possible to impose the semantic structure it finds in that language on any other. It may be marginally useful to add these two remarks: the fact that the underlying semantic structure of one language will serve for all is a purely conceptual point which depends on what counts as translation. The second remark is: it is encouraging to reflect that just about everything of philosophical interest in the study of meaning will emerge if we stick to the case that is nearest home, a theory for English couched in English. But it would be a mistake to confuse such a theory with a universal theory of meaning.

Now I turn to my central topic, a program for a theory of meaning for English. What should we demand of such a theory? Well, at least this: the theory should give the meaning of every meaningful expression. The problem is to interpret this demand in a viable way. Since there is no clear limit to the number of meaningful expressions, a workable theory must account for the meaning of each expression on the basis of the patterned exhibition of a finite number of features. But even if there were a practical constraint on the length of sentences a person can send and receive with understanding, a satisfactory semantics would need to explain the contribution of repeatable features to the meaning of the sentences in which they occur.

I suggest that a theory of truth does, in a minimal but very important way, do what is needed, that is, give the meanings of all independently meaningful expressions on the basis of their structure. And on the other hand, no theory of meaning can be considered adequate unless it provides an account of the concept of truth. It is not part of my plan to argue that a theory of truth is a complete theory of meaning; I shall be happy if I can persuade you that a complete theory must contain, or entail, a theory of truth, and that a theory of truth goes much further in meeting reasonable demands on a theory of meaning than is generally realized. I also hope it will become clear that a theory of the kind I shall outline provides an insight into the nature of language; that it reconciles, up to a point at least, a desire to describe accurately the language we actually use, on the one hand, with a bent for system and logic on the other; and that it can illuminate a number of questions from various branches of philosophy. Theory of truth, as I conceive it, provides a framework for asking certain questions in philosophy, a methodology for answering them or at any rate a range of methods, and a clear criterion of success within the limits of the discipline. Not that I think we now have found the one right way of doing philosophy. It would be fairer to say that a theory of truth pulls together, in a usefully self-conscious and explicit way, techniques and criteria for the analysis of language that have been used by philosophers of almost every period and school. While I am listing the virtues of the idea let me say finally that I do not see how a descriptive theory can be considered complete unless it includes a theory of truth. It seems to me inescapable that the semantic structure uncovered by a theory of truth will correspond to the deep structure postulated by an intuitively satisfactory syntax; but I realize that some who know far more than I do about the problems of syntax do not share this conviction.

It is popular nowadays to stress the creative aspects of language, the fact that someone who can speak or decipher a language can cope with sentences he has never heard. This is usually taken, and I think rightly, to imply that to grasp a language is to deal with it as a recursive structure. The point is usually made with respect to syntax, whose primary and only clear concern is with sentencehood or meaningfulness. But the more important requirement is a recursive semantics, whose concern is with truth and meaning. Indeed, it might be argued that if we had an adequate theory of meaning, what was left for syntax would be a relatively trivial subject. A theory of meaning we may imagine to assign a meaning to the grammatical and ungrammatical alike, but to provide no official clue to the line between; what would remain for syntax would then be the drawing of this line.

It will help bring out the nature of a recursive semantics to adopt for a moment a Fregean outlook. Frege thought of the theory of a language as consisting of two interlocking parts, a theory of truth and reference on the one hand, and a theory of sense or meaning on the other. To make my simple contrast I shall ignore the interlocking, and much else that is important in Frege: I want to show how incomplete the parallel between the two parts of the theory really is.

Frege's central idea was to read every sentence as composed (essentially) of syntactic features that correspond to functions and syntactic features that correspond to singular terms. On the side of reference, the functions map extensions, one or more, onto extensions, and finally onto a truth value, which is the extension or reference of a sentence. On the side of sense, the functions map senses (intensions, meanings), one or more, onto senses, and finally onto a proposition, which is the intension or sense of a sentence. The central task of theory of reference could be conceived as that of defining a function $t(\bar{s}) = T$ mapping sentences onto truth values, the task of theory of sense or meaning is that of defining a function $m(\bar{s}) = M$ mapping sentences onto propositions. And now I can state the contrast I have in mind: we know, from the work of Frege and Tarski, how to give a nontrivial definition of the function $t(\bar{s}) = T$, while we have no idea how to take even the first step in defining m($\bar{s}$) = M. Take an example. The reference of the sentential connective "or" in the sentence "Socrates is wise or Xanthippe is beautiful" is a function that maps pairs of truth values onto a truth value. So t("Socrates is wise or Xanthippe is beautiful") = T if and only if t("Socrates is wise") = T or t("Xanthippe is beautiful") = T. The sense of "or" is a function that maps pairs of senses (propositions) onto a sense. But assuming we know the sense of "Socrates is wise" and the sense of "Xanthippe is beautiful," what is the value of m("Socrates is wise or Xanthippe is beautiful")? The answer we are apt to get is: the sense of "Socrates is wise or Xanthippe is beautiful," but the answer has the form of "x = x" and so cannot be used to suggest how a theory of meaning based on senses could be constructed. The present objection to meanings or propositions in the theory of meaning has nothing to do with their supposed obscurity, but with their failure to serve the purpose at hand.

The point is fundamental, and yet it is easy to miss. Take a simplest case, a sentence consisting of a proper name and a predicate. How can we give the value of the truth function for "Socrates is wise"? It can be given thus: t("Socrates is wise") = T if and only if Socrates is wise. This answer has struck many people as being so trivial as to be no answer at all. But it is a step toward appreciating the formula which our biconditional exemplifies to contrast it with what can be done for the sense of "Socrates is wise." Our biconditional gives the value of t for the argument "Socrates is wise" without using the concept of truth, indeed without using any conceptual devices not contained in the sentence whose truth value is at stake. As far as I can see, there is no analogous formula for a theory of sense.

It is if anything easier to see why a theory that does no more than provide a translation or paraphrase (or set of paraphrases) for every sentence fails to provide what is basic to a theory of meaning. The fact that such theories may make use of a recursively given syntactic theory does not alter matters. They still define no function of the kind we seek: they define instead the independent concept of synonymy, as within the language, or between languages. But one can know what pairs of sentences are synonymous without having any idea what they mean, much less how their meaning depends on the semantic significance of their parts and structure. A clear sign that a theory of paraphrase falls short of being a theory of meaning is that it can give no systematic account of entailment relations between sentences. A semantics based on syntax plus a lexicon (elaborated, perhaps, in terms of semantic markers and selection restrictions) can be made to implement trivial entailments of the "unmarried male"—"bachelor" variety; where it will fail is in distinguishing, say, between opaque and transparent contexts—contexts in which substitutability of identity works, and those where it fails. The deep difference between semantics based on theory of truth and semantics as it is often understood by transformational linguists today emerges clearly at this point. For only a theory of truth can serve as a foundation for the study of entailment relations.

A moment ago I described, in rough outline, Frege's conception of a theory of truth in order to compare it favorably with his parallel conception of a theory of sense. The theory I sketched was not, as everyone knows, quite Frege's, and it is not mine either. I simplified and distorted Frege by having functional expressions, like "the father of" and, in Frege's opinion, "or" and "is wise," refer to functions. But now I should like to abandon this view in favor of the view that no entity at all corresponds to such expressions. What is attractive about Frege's theory does not depend on finding entities, complete or incomplete, to answer to these expressions, but rather the idea that the truth value of a sentence can be defined to depend systematically on these expressions and on what simple singular terms refer to. The first step in ridding Frege of unnecessary ontology is to dispense with truth values as objects named by sentences. If we can define a function $t(\bar{s}) = T$ then we can as easily define a predicate "is true"; in fact we will already have done so, for we can simply take all but the "$\bar{s}$" in "$t(\bar{s}) = T$" as a one-place predicate true of sentences. This change will make us give up treating sentential connectives literally as truth *functions*, for no entities will be left to serve as arguments. But no matter, for we can easily enough say when a complex sentence is true on the basis of the truth or falsity of the components. Similarly for functional expressions and ordinary predicates: Frege's ontological machinery got us to thinking in terms of a recursive theory, which is good, and it has its uses in pressing analogies when intensional contexts are under consideration. But for the analysis of ordinary extensional contexts, the ontological apparatus is excess baggage—except, of course, for the entities to which genuine singular terms refer, and the entities over which the variables of quantification range.

Of these departures from Frege, the important one is giving up the idea that in the theory of truth there must be an entity corresponding to a predicate. A Fregean theory states the circumstances under which a simple sentence is true (i.e. names the true) in some such way as this:

t("Socrates is wise") = T iff the function associated with "is wise" maps the entity named by "Socrates" onto the True.

This statement requires two semantical notions, that of naming, and that of a function mapping an argument onto the True. The first of these notions might be explicitly defined in turn, but the entity it brings in, namely Socrates, will have to be in the ontology when the time comes to give an account of quantification—for example in giving the truth conditions of "Socrates exists." But if the other semantic concept is defined, then the entity corresponding to the predicate is shown to be superfluous. So we may say, about any such theory of truth, that the entities it postulates as corresponding to predicates are not really needed, or else it contains an irreducible semantic primitive not required by some other theories.

The issues over which I have just brushed—the ontological implication of a theory of truth—will come in for more attention in my next lecture. My concern now is to emphasize the importance of sentences like "The sentence 'Socrates is wise' is true iff Socrates is wise." A Fregean theory, I have just remarked, does not entail sentences of this form unless it at the same time demonstrates that part of the theory is idle. I assume that a Fregean will deny that an important part of his theory does no work; he will presumably choose instead to give up the crucial connection between his theory and sentences like " 'Socrates is wise' is true iff Socrates is wise."

I shall take the opposite course. It seems to me that there are good reasons for being interested in theories that assign a central role to sentences of the form "s̄ is true iff s." These reasons are easy to state in outline.

From here on I am going to call a sentence that instantiates the form "s̄ is true iff s" a T-sentence. The first point about T-sentences is that each such sentence fixes the extension of the predicate "is true" at one point, that is, with respect to one sentence; if Socrates is wise, then the sentence "Socrates is wise" belongs to the extension of the predicate "is true," otherwise not. Since there is a T-sentence for every sentence of the language, the totality of T-sentences precisely determines the extension of the predicate "is true," assuming, of course, that the class of sentences has been settled.

Clearly, then, a theory that entails every T-sentence will satisfy one obvious demand on an adequate theory of truth. But is a theory that meets the test necessarily of any interest? Suppose a theory entailed all T-sentences simply by enumerating all the truths. Such a theory would throw no light on meaning at all: we could know what sentences were true without knowing what any meant. The possibility of such a theory need not worry us, needless to say, since one cannot be provided even for elementary number theory. A serious difficulty is raised, however, by the fact that since the totality of T-sentences is easy to characterize syntactically (at least for the case where the metalanguage includes the object language), the T-sentences themselves might all be taken as axioms of the theory. This would yield a correct and utterly frivolous theory (this does seem to be the very theory many critics of the semantic approach to truth have thought was typical). The most obvious, though perhaps not the most perceptive, way to forestall such trivialization is to insist that the theory contain only a finite number of non-logical axioms. The effect of this constraint is to ensure that an account of the truth conditions for all sentences of a language must show how the truth of a sentence depends on a recursive structure or form.

A striking feature of a T-sentence is that it gives the truth conditions of a sentence using no conceptual resources not in the sentence itself. If a sentence contains a reference to a semantical notion, or a set, or a dog, then its T-sentence gives its truth conditions by referring to a semantical notion, or a set, or a dog; but not otherwise. Thus the semantical notion of truth is, so to speak, washed away a sentence at a time by T-sentences. This is why Tarski says that a theory (or definition) of truth is no more than the "logical product" of all T-sentences. The criterion of an adequate theory that we have been using—roughly, that it consists of a finite set of axioms entailing all T-sentences (which is approximately Tarski's Convention T)—is in one way an apparently weak demand on a theory of meaning. On the other hand, I am suggesting that it also requires something profound and in a way maximal: that the theory give an account of a fundamental semantic notion, truth, using only the resources available in the language for which truth is being characterized. If the truth predicate itself were in that language, the language would be contradictory. What Convention T sets as a condition is not that the truth predicate be in the object language, but that the resources used to characterize it be.

What I have just said is imprecise and even inaccurate, but it helps give the spirit of the enterprise. It is true that a theory adequate by the standard of Convention T tends (as I said in discussing Frege) to make redundant appeal to semantic concepts (besides those it recursively characterizes), and it is a merit of Convention T to help us see why. But it is too much to say that we can prove that any theory that satisfies the criterion must have all the depth and interest of the theories we are familiar with. I can only claim that the known theories have these merits, and theories that do not satisfy Convention T do not.

I have been stressing the fact that the T-sentences of a language exactly fix the extension of the truth predicate, and do so in an interesting way. I have been assuming that they fix it correctly. This is trivially so in the simplest case where the metalanguage is nothing but the language to be studied plus one or two new predicates ("satisfied," "is true"). But this simplest case will yield to many complications, and as it does so the question when a T-sentence is true will become pressing. One obvious complication emerges when truth is relativized to the circumstances of utterance, as it clearly must be. I have been blithely ignoring this fact for some tens of minutes and talking as if we could treat truth as a property of sentences. We know this is impossible: we must treat it either as an attribute of statements (what is said by the use of a sentence on occasion) or as a relation between a speaker and a sentence (tense, pronoun, demonstrative) whose truth conditions are being given. The T-sentence must be supplemented with an expression that fixes the reference relative to the circumstance of utterance. For example, the sentence "You will recover" is true relative to a speaker and a time iff the person addressed by the speaker at that time will recover after that time.

A more subtle change in the character of T-sentences comes when the assumption that the language under study is identical with part of the language used for expressing the results of the study is dropped. The assumption is of course dropped if one language is, say, Sherpa and the other is English; but it is also dropped as *mere* assumption when one person formulates (explicitly or in the heat of dispute) a theory about what his supposed co-linguist means by what he says.

The idea that wants emphasis now, however, applies even to the most obvious case of translation: T-sentences are as easy to judge true or false as anything that could count as evidence for the correctness of a theory of meaning. For, as remarked, they contain no semantic vocabulary (except for the truth predicate), no reference to logical form, no general laws. To recognize them as true, we require no insight into synonymy, deep structure, or meanings. Yet there is nothing more to the question whether a theory of truth is correct than the question whether the T-sentences it entails are true. So it seems that a theory of truth satisfying Convention T, though it yields, if I am right, important and by no means obvious results about a language, can be tested by appeal to knowledge plausibly explicit to a native speaker, and as available as any to the radical translator or descriptive linguist.

Some linguists ask that an adequate theory reflect the "internalized grammar" of speakers of the language. Chomsky in particular has argued that the superiority of transformational grammars over others lies in the fact that transformational grammars can be made to "correspond to the linguistic intuition of the native speaker." The problem is to find a relatively clear test of when a theory corresponds to a speaker's linguistic intuition. I suggest that we can give empirical bite to this idea if we identify deep structure with the form a theory of truth assigns to a sentence (logical form). I will illustrate by commenting on a passage in Chomsky.

Chomsky says that the following two sentences, though they have the same surface structure, differ in deep structure:

(1) I persuaded John to leave.
(2) I expected John to leave.

The demonstration rests chiefly on the observation that when an embedded sentence in a sentence somewhat like (2) is transformed to the passive, the result is "cognitively synonymous" with the active form; but a similar transformation does not yield a synonymous result for the analogue of (1). The observation is clearly correct, but how does it show that (1) and (2) have radically different deep structures? At most the evidence suggests that a theory that assigns different structures to (1) and (2) may be simpler than one that does not. But how our linguistic intuitions have been tapped to prove a difference here is certainly obscure.

But of course Chomsky is right; there is a contrast between (1) and (2), and it emerges dramatically the moment we start thinking in terms of constructing a theory of truth. Indeed, we need go no further than to ask about the semantic role of the word "John" in both sentences. In (1), "John" can be replaced by any co-referring term without altering the truth value of (1); this is not true of (2). The contribution of the word "John" to the truth condition of (1) must therefore be radically different from its contribution to the truth conditions of (2). This way of showing there is a difference in the semantic structure of (1) and (2) requires no appeal to "the speaker's tacit knowledge" of the grammar or the "intrinsic competence of the idealized native speaker." It rests on the *explicit* knowledge any speaker of English has of the way in which (1) and (2) may vary in truth under substitutions for the word "John."

Yet these last remarks do not do justice to the method of truth. They show that by bearing the requirements of a theory of truth in mind we can throw into relief, perhaps more plainly than Chomsky succeeds in doing, our feeling of a difference in structure between (1) and (2). So far, though, the evidence to which we are appealing is of much the same sort as Chomsky uses: mainly questions of the loss or preservation of truth value under transformations. Such considerations will no doubt continue to guide the constructive and analytic labors of linguists as they long have those of philosophers. The beauty of a theory of the sort we have been discussing is that these intimations of structure, however useful or essential they may be to the discovery of a suitable theory, need play no direct role in testing the final product. For it can be tested, as we have seen, simply by asking whether the T-sentences it entails are true.

Lecture II
Truth and Ontology (May 15, 1970)

The systematic study of the conditions under which someone speaks the truth must throw light on the question of what exists. I would like to explore some of the consequences for ontology of a theory of truth that satisfies Tarski's Convention T suitably modified to apply to a natural language. The essence of the requirement is that an adequate theory must be stated using only a finite number of non-logical axioms and must entail all T-sentences, which we may for a bit longer think of as having the form of " 'Snow is white' is true iff snow is white."

Sentences in this form are ontologically neutral. After it is relativized to a speaker and other circumstances of utterance, the basic predicate "is true" applies to such entities as sentences, or without relativization to utterances, speech acts, or statements, but it does not relate these entities or events to something else "in the world" that they might be thought to be about. I don't mean that the sentence on the right of the biconditional used to give truth conditions may not have an ontological burden, but that this burden is not owed to the analysis of truth as such, only to the analysis of the sentence. There *are* theories that relate sentences or utterances or statements to entities like states of affairs or facts; I'll consider them presently, but a theory that satisfies Convention T does not.

A theory that satisfies Convention T (let me call it a *T-theory*, perhaps for Tarski, perhaps for Truth) is in fact startlingly free from apparent ontological encumbrances. It gives up Frege's idea that sentences name truth values in favor of treating the basic truth locution ("is true") as an unstructured predicate, and it gives up, at least at the start, the idea that predicates and functional expressions require any corresponding entities at all for the theory to operate. Not only are these extensional entities dispensed with but so also are intensional entities: meanings or propositions. A T-theory of truth, if I am right, does much of what we legitimately want of a theory of meaning; in particular it shows how the meaning of a sentence depends on the meanings of the parts, at least in this sense, that it accounts for the conditions under which a sentence is true on the basis of its semantically

The Structure of Truth: The 1970 John Locke Lectures. Cameron Domenico Kirk-Giannini and Ernie Lepore, Oxford University Press (2020). © Cameron Domenico Kirk-Giannini and Ernie Lepore.
DOI: 10.1093/oso/9780198842491.001.0001

relevant structure. But it does this without finding a use for entities that could be called meanings. A theory of truth constructed along the lines proposed by Tarski seems, then, to tell us nothing interesting about ontology.

The appearance of ontological triviality is deceptive, but it is instructive to notice that it springs from the same source as the popular view that semantic theories of truth are in general, as J. L. Austin put it, "a series of truisms." The common source is the *form* of T-sentences, which tell us what a theory must do, for each T-sentence may (with reservations that will emerge) be considered a truism, and a theory of truth may be thought of, to use Tarski's own phrase, as the "logical product" of the T-sentences. What difference is there, after all, between the logical product of a set of truisms and a "series" of truisms? I think we must agree that *if* the theory of truth is nothing but the totality of T-sentences, it is ontologically barren, and yields no insight into the semantic structure of the language. But we have ruled the antecedent false by ruling out the possibility of taking each T-sentence as a postulate. So an adequate theory will necessarily present a recursive analysis of the semantic features of every sentence, an analysis that reveals *more than can be guessed* from the T-sentence for that sentence, or from the totality of T-sentences.

Before trying to explain in more detail how a theory of truth can clarify the ontological assumptions of a language I want to pick up a large loose end that is concerned with ontology in a different way—the question what entities, if any, are properly called true and false: the subject matter of our inquiry.

A theory of truth is a theory *about* the speech behavior of one or more people. The group to whom the theory applies cannot be *independently* characterized as the speakers of some language; rather, to say the theory applies to them is to assert that they do speak the language. To identify a language is therefore to identify a theory; the concept of a language is not a concept that can occur *within* a theory of truth; there is no room in the theory for expressing the idea that the theory as a whole applies to one speaker or group rather than another.

What we must bear in mind, then, is that phrases like "true-in-English" or "true-for-the-inhabitants-of-this-town"or "true-in-Davidson's-language" cannot be treated as logically composed of a predicate "true" with one of its places filled with a name or description. At first this feature of the semantic approach to truth (which is forced by the semantic paradoxes) may seem to create intolerable problems; for example, it would seem to prevent us from making sense of such a statement as "Mohammed and Christ both said many true things." I shall try later to give a natural solution to this, and associated, difficulties.

My main purpose now, however, is to distinguish the sense in which a theory of truth is a theory about a particular speaker (or group) from a sense in which truth *within* the theory, and hence within the language of which it is the theory, *is* relative to a speaker. This latter kind of relativity is to accommodate the fact that one and the same sentence may be true when spoken by one person and false when spoken by another though both speak the same language. This must be counted a feature of the language even if the language is spoken by only one person: my theory of your language would be defective if I counted the word "I" as naming you, even if no one else spoke your language, for *if* someone else did, his "I" would refer to him. Actually, there are reasons for not being happy with the word "refer" here, and we do not need it. The T-sentence for "I am standing" should come out something like " 'I am standing' is true for a speaker at a time if the speaker is standing at that time," and here the notion of reference does not appear.

As the last example made plain, truth must be relativized to the time of utterance as well as the speaker if tenses and other time-indexical expressions (like "tomorrow") are to be treated with proper respect. Perhaps it will ward off misunderstanding to make two comments on the simple treatment of the tenses I am outlining. One is that it is not, in itself, a *logic* of tense, it only aims to give an account of the conditions under which tensed statements are true. And, a second point, it certainly does not provide, or aim to provide, a tenseless paraphrase or substitute for tensed sentences. There are no general, non-indexical, substitutes for indexical expressions and sentences.

Perhaps we can imagine the following: a man might speak the sound "Nein" into the telephone intending his mistress, who is on the other end of the line, and speaks English, to expect him at nine, and intending his wife, who is in the room, and speaks German, to understand that he will not be at home for supper. A theory that covered the case would apparently have to make truth relative not only to the speaker and the time, but also to the intended audience. The issue raised by the example is important, for it casts in doubt the view that the theory a speaker has for his own speech has to be shared by a hearer for communication to take place. I won't try to resolve this puzzle; the question may be left open for present purposes.

Is further relativization necessary? I don't think so. Of course indexical expressions refer to other things than the time of utterance and the speaker, but in each case what is indicated is a function of the time and speaker.

So "That button is loose" is true for a speaker and a time if the button the speaker indicates at that time is loose, "Tomorrow will be windy" is true if the day after it is spoken is windy, and "I caught a fish this long" is true if sometime prior to the utterance the speaker caught a fish as long as the distance indicated by the speaker at the time of utterance. The basic concept with which a theory of meaning works is, I have been suggesting, that of a speaker speaking the literal truth in uttering a sentence at a particular time. The notion of literal truth is, to remind you of the theme of my first lecture, the one we use if we say that a man has spoken the truth without knowing it, and intending to lie; or if we allow that someone might intend to exaggerate and yet hit on the truth; or if we say a man may speak the truth in remarking of Jones that he was burned up, meaning that Jones was angry when he was in fact consumed by flames. And now I want to introduce a slight change in the basic concept, I want to retain, as the aim of the theory, the positive and constructive description of the kind of truth that depends on what words literally mean when spoken on specific occasions. But an adjustment is needed because a sentence may be true for a speaker at a time even if he does not speak it. If an English speaker utters the words "Socrates flies" and he speaks the truth, then Socrates flies; but not conversely, since Socrates may fly and no one speak.

This difficulty can be met by taking truth to be a relation between a sentence, a speaker, and a time that holds whether or not the speaker speaks that sentence at that time. When this relation holds, the sentence is *acceptable* for the speaker, in this sense: if he believed what the sentence expresses for him, he would have a true belief.

The (new) basic truth relation is connected with speaking the truth in a simple way: if a sentence is true at a time for a speaker, *and* he utters that sentence, then he speaks the truth. This shows how the concept of speaking the truth can be defined in terms of the basic truth relation. It is tempting to try the reverse course. Why not say that the basic truth relation between a sentence, speaker, and time holds provided the speaker would have spoken the truth had he uttered the sentence at the time? The difficulty, which had not occurred to me until David Kaplan forced it to my attention, is seen in this example: the sentence "I am now silent" is true for a person when he is silent. But even at such a time it would be false *if* he were to utter it.

The absurdities that follow if truth is conceived as a property of sentences have obviously been circumvented. In theories of the kind under consideration, the truth predicate is relational, and so cannot represent a property of anything, much less of sentences. If we were to seek an entity to which to attribute a property, a natural one to choose would be an ordered triple consisting of a sentence, a person, and a date; such a triple could be said to have the *property* of truth when the truth *relation* held between the three items of the triple. Utterances, tokens, inscriptions, speech acts correspond in obvious ways to certain of these triples, and some of them to the true triples, so by a natural extension we could say of these utterances, tokens, inscriptions, or speech acts that *they* possessed the simple property of truth. These are various pieces of linguistic legislation we could pass if it pleased us, but unless the proposals come close to some common idiom, I can think of nothing to recommend them. When people object to saying that utterances, say, are true or false, I'm not sure what worries them. If the claim is merely that we don't talk that way, it is probably for the most part true. But if the claim is that it is wrong, or actively misleading, to talk that way, then I have yet to hear the reasons. On the contrary, it seems to me obvious what a philosopher means who says that utterances are vehicles of truth, and I see nothing wrong with his language, except that it isn't quite English.

A different, and more difficult, issue is raised by the view that it is statements, propositions, or things said that are properly called true and false. Part of the trouble is easy to explain away. If exception be taken to saying the sentence " 'Snow is white' is at all times true for Jones" it may be that one of the following seems better: "The statement expressed by the sentence 'Snow is white' is always true for Jones" or "The sentence 'Snow is white' always expresses a true statement so far as Jones is concerned." The revised sentences seem to contain a singular term, "the statement expressed by sentence s when spoken by so-and-so at such-and-such a time," that contains a functor mapping triples consisting of a sentence, a speaker, and a time onto a statement; and then truth is treated as a property of statements. Statements so conceived work just as the ordered triples from which they sprang—we are back where we were a page or so ago. But the more important point is that all this apparatus is idle unless we have some further need for statements, unless there are things we can say, by treating statements as independent entities, that we cannot say as well by talking simply of sentences, speakers, and occasions. [Let me put this a slightly different way. Consider the sentence:

The statement expressed by "Snow is white" is true for Jones right now.

There are three singular terms, "Snow is white," "Jones," and "right now"; the rest is predicate. This predicate might need further breaking up into a singular term ("the statement expressed by…") and a one-place predicate ("is true"), or it might not. No amount of staring at this sentence will tell us; it all depends on what other sentences containing the words "statement" and "true" there are, and how they are related to the one before us. So for the present at least we can have the *syntax* of statement-description and one-place truth-predicate without an *ontology* of statements or a property of truth.]

The standing apparatus of a theory of truth that satisfies Convention T requires, then, at least three categories of entities: sentences (which are, of course abstract things—shapes, perhaps); people; and times. (These last will yield in the end to events and numbers.) It is time to return to the question what further entities must exist if particular sentences are true, according to the theory.

It will quicken our appreciation of T-theories to sketch the ontological implications of some alternatives. Consider first what we may call the double-negation theory of truth. According to this view the words "It is true that…" when prefixed to a sentence should be treated as an operator with the properties of double-negation: the result of prefixing the words to a sentence is true if the sentence is, otherwise false. (The analogy with double-negation may break down if the truth-operator is prefixed to a sentence without a truth value.) The double-negation theory will work as well for the truth locutions in "The statement that ____ is true," "____, and that's the truth," "It is true to the facts to say that ____." And clearly, the double-negation theory has no ontological implications whatever. It even is inimical to statements, for in "the statement that Socrates is wise is true" the words "The statement that Socrates is wise" cannot constitute a singular term without, contrary to the theory, turning "is true" into a predicate.

The double-negation theory is unacceptable because it provides no account of the role of the words "is true" in such a sentence as "Fermat's last theorem is true" or "I can't remember what it was, but the last thing you said was true."

Defenders of the idea that talk of truth is redundant often slip at this point to a different theory. The motivation is easy to follow. If we knew what Fermat's last theorem was we could avoid talk of truth—we could simply speak the theorem. Not knowing it, why can't we say something like, whatever statement Fermat's last theorem may be, I make it. Truth may still tremble in that last phrase, but the following symbolism seems to show how to avoid it:

(1)   (p) (the statement that p = Fermat's last theorem → p)

Here there is open acceptance of statements as entities, since phrases describing them flank an identity sign. The variable, however, doesn't range over statements, but over whatever it is that we are assuming sentences to name. I think there is a good argument to show that this device, contrary to appearances, does not really eliminate the concept of truth. Frege showed, relying on natural assumptions, that if sentences name anything, all the true ones must name the same thing (I'll give this argument presently). Looking at our analysis of "Fermat's last theorem is true" we see that Frege's result comes to showing that there is only one true statement. So given the proposal, "Fermat's last theorem is true" is equivalent to "Fermat's last theorem = *the* true statement"—the quantification over statements is idle since there are only two things to quantify over (the true and the false). But now we have a truth-predicate in the words "is identical with the true statement," and one that might well be shortened to "is true."

Ramsey apparently thought it would be possible to give a recursive account of the conditions under which a statement was true that would permit systematic elimination of truth-words, but he unfortunately did not carry out the recursion. If he *had* he might well have discovered the semantic theory of truth. But it is a safe guess that when he was done he would no longer have clung to the view that the concept of truth is trivial. Nor would the claim that the concept of truth is redundant survive. For although a recursive theory of truth can be turned into an explicit definition by familiar methods, and so a substitute for the truth predicate can be provided that is not specifically semantical, this cannot be done by using only the concepts and ontology of the language for which the truth predicate is defined.

Theories that attempt to explain the truth of a statement by postulating a *fact* or *state of affairs* to which it corresponds would seem to be theories that require an interesting ontology. But is this really so? Facts are interesting and have potential explanatory power to the extent that we can describe them in ways that do not depend directly on the sentences or statements whose truth facts are to explain. It would be a sign of the independence of facts from language if the fact described by a term was not altered if in that term a singular term were replaced by a co-referring one. Suppose it is a fact that Odysseus visited the palace of King Alcinous and Queen Arete and suppose it is true that this palace is the one whose remains are now to be seen above the modern town of Paleokastritsa. Then the fact that Odysseus visited the palace of King Alcinous and Queen Arete should be identical with the fact that Odysseus visited the palace whose remains are now to be seen above the modern town of Paleokastritsa. The principle of identity we have accepted here, coupled with the principle that logically equivalent sentences can be substituted in fact descriptions without changing the description, lead to the conclusion that all (true) facts are identical. The argument, which is Frege's, can take this form: if s and t are any two true sentences, then the class of objects that are (self-identical and such that s) is identical with the class of objects that are (self-identical and such that t) (both are the universal class). Consider the fact that [the class of objects that are (self-identical and such that s) is the universal class]; this is the same fact as the fact that [the class of objects that are (self-identical and such that t) is the universal class]. But the sentence embedded in the first fact-description is logically equivalent with s, and the sentence embedded in the second fact-description is logically equivalent with t. So the fact that s is identical with the fact that t. But all we know about s and t is that both are true. If there is only one fact, then when we want to say a statement is true we need only say it corresponds to The Fact ("the facts" is more generous than necessary). Ontological interest once more fades; if there is only one fact to which a statement can correspond, we explain no more, and say no more, when we say a sentence corresponds to The Fact than when we simply say that it is true.

Frege's argument may be defeated in a number of ways: by not allowing class abstraction as primitive, or by denying the principle of substitutivity of identity, or by not accepting the principle that logically equivalent sentences correspond to the same fact. Any of these courses reduces the chances for a non-trivial description of the fact that verifies a statement. And it is significant that any of these courses prevents the straightforward construction of a theory of truth that satisfies Convention T.

We have not quite demonstrated that a theory of truth based on correspondence to facts is impossible, or even that it might not be instructive. One familiar strategy involves first explaining what it is for a simple sentence consisting of an n-place predicate with its predicate places filled with proper names to correspond to a fact. Next, truth (or corresponding to a fact, if there are complex facts) for truth-functionally complex sentences is explained in the obvious way on the basis of the truth of the atomic sentences. Finally, quantificational truth is explained in terms of truth of the atomic sentences or the existence of appropriate atomic facts.

One difficulty with this story is to get it started, to give a plausible account of the relation of correspondence between atomic sentence and atomic fact. Assuming there are a finite number of names and of simple predicates, it could be done by enumerating the cases: "Socrates is wise" corresponds to the fact that Socrates is wise ↔ Socrates is wise; but this merely shows how to get along without facts. The harder, but more interesting, way is to attempt a real insight into correspondence, for example in terms of *picturing*. I shall discuss this idea, which seems to me to fail, in my next lecture.

The other major difficulty is in explaining quantification. One might try this: a universal quantification of a predicate, say "x is left-handed," is true just in case every fact of a certain kind exists. What kind, exactly? It does not seem possible to say without quantifying over, not only facts, but also left-handed entities; and if this is done it will be as easy to define truth for such sentences *without* recourse to facts.

It's hard to get any work out of facts, for the other possibility is simply to give the truth conditions for quantified sentences in terms of the truth of instances, and this is again to demonstrate that facts are excess baggage.

I shall now give up on facts: I think they are a dead end so far as serious semantics are concerned. I have spent this much time on the idea because it helps illustrate my present thesis, which is that only a theory of truth that satisfies convention T can be counted on to give us real instruction about how language is related to the world, and this seems to me a point of the very greatest importance for philosophy of language, and for philosophy generally.

A lead has opened up that is independent of facts—the substitutional analysis of quantification. As an approach to truth, it is simply this: the existential quantification of an open sentence is true if there is a true sentence gotten by deleting the quantifier and replacing the variable by a singular term; a universal quantification of an open sentence is true if every replacement of the quantifier variable by a singular term results in a true sentence. Assuming it is possible to define truth for atomic sentences and connectives, this promises to be a way to characterize truth in general (for a particular speaker or language, of course).

What makes substitutional quantification so interesting is that it suggests that we can divorce questions of truth and meaning on the one hand from questions of ontology on the other. If we can do theory of meaning and truth without ontology, then the idea that we can learn something about ontology by studying language will lose any plausibility it may have had. It is going to occur to any good empiricist that ontology is the bunk—the objects we suppose our sentences to be about are nothing but the shadows of certain parts of speech, and shadows we do not need in explaining truth. Truth itself is not a relation between a statement and something the statement is about, or so at least I have been arguing. But then, if we can explain truth for basic sentences without explicit ontology (and we can if the vocabulary is finite and we do not allow complex singular terms), and can explain truth for the other cases as depending on truth for the basic sentences, then we have shown how to do semantics without (ordinary) ontology. On such a theory, sentences would have semantically significant structure, but there would be no drawing ontological conclusions from the details of the structure.

It is an attractive vision in many ways. It encourages us to think of our language as a whole much as the formalists viewed mathematics—a machine for getting from truth to truth without touching things. Problems of existence vanish: we needn't worry about universals, numbers, sets, electrons, diseases, or cats and dogs. We needn't worry about any *thing*.

Substitutional quantification does not have to wear so extreme a face. It is a theory about the semantics of quantifiers, and if it worked it would show that quantification as such involved no ontology not already introduced by singular terms. A theory of the semantics of singular terms, if there are an infinite number of them, cannot remain so pure. Consider a language with the sentence "Socrates is wise" and all the sentences gotten by prefixing a sentence by the words "the father of." A recursive account of truth for this mini-language would have to begin by characterizing a relation of denotation, thus: "Socrates" denotes Socrates, and the result of writing "the father of" in front of an expression x denotes the father of the entity denoted by x. The rule for truth is: a sentence consisting of the words "Socrates is wise" with zero or more occurrences of "The father of" in front is true if the entity denoted by the words preceding "is wise" is wise.

I want to say, the substitutionalist's ontology is now showing, for in explaining truth he has had to quantify, in the metalanguage, over entities denoted by expressions in the object language. But of course he will reply, if he is interested in remaining uncommitted, that his view from the start was that quantification as such has no consequences for ontology, and if this holds for the object language it must hold for the metalanguage. Pursuing the matter, we should look again at the substitutionalist's account of quantification. Let us add to our little language which discourses on the wisdom of Socrates' patrilineal ancestors sentences obtained from the original supply by writing "(∃x)" in front and replacing "Socrates" and any number of occurrences of "the father of" by "x." Clearly a given existentially quantified sentence can be obtained in this way from any of a denumerably large class of unquantified sentences. And now for the semantic rule: an existentially quantified sentence is true if at least one of the sentences from which it can be obtained is true.

It is often said, and with justice, that this rule is wrong, if the [existential] quantifier is to mean what we normally mean by such phrases as "There exists something such that" or "There is someone who" or just "Someone" as in "Someone is wise." For, the complaint goes, it may be true that someone is wise and yet that neither Socrates, nor his father, nor his father's father,... is wise. The objection here depends on someone not being in the family (on the father's side). The case is special, since the patrilineal line is (at most) denumerable and we can see that everyone in it has his singular term. Whenever we can order the entities in a series, we can make substitutional quantification work—indeed, as Quine and others have pointed out, we can use the numerals as the names, or even take the numbers to be the only entities. The real difficulty arises when we suppose the totality of things is not denumerable, or that there is no way to map them onto the natural numbers.

Still, what have we shown? Only that substitutional quantification, with its ontological neutrality, *may* be false, not that it is. The number of entities in the universe may not be denumerable—but who knows? If it is denumerable, then for all our argument shows, there may as well be nothing. Quine has taken the point very much to heart. Since no amount of evidence can show that someone else is not operating with a substitutional scheme, the ontology of others is forever beyond us; and language being the social instrument it is, to admit this is to allow that we can make no ultimate sense of the idea that a person may commit himself to the existence of an object by what he says.

Much—everything, we might say—hangs on whether we can show substitutional quantification inadequate. I think we can. Our trouble a moment ago was that we could easily see that the substitutional theory *might* give the wrong result, but we couldn't see that it must. What we forgot was that an adequate theory must *entail* a proper T-sentence for each sentence of the object language. And surely it is a defect in a theory if it does not show that if "Someone is wise" is true, then someone is wise. Yet the substitutional theory does fail to imply this. According to our toy theory (which reflects the real thing well enough), if "Someone is wise" is true, then some sentence of the form "___ is wise" is true, with the blank filled by a singular term. But the theory provides no way to go from this to the conclusion that someone is wise. It is no help that in the metalanguage we can infer "Someone is wise" from "Socrates is wise," for there is no way to reach "Socrates is wise" from the premise "The sentence 'Someone is wise' is true." Everything would go like clockwork if we added as a premise the assumption that every singular term denotes someone; and the converse argument would succeed if we made explicit the assumption that everyone is denoted by some singular term. These assumptions destroy, however, what was interesting about substitutional quantification, for they make the ontological character of quantification explicit. (I owe much of this argument to John Wallace.)

The objection, then, to substitutional quantification is that it fails to yield this as a consequence: if what we are taking as an existential quantification in the object language is true, then something exists. What we *know* to be existential quantification in our own language doesn't suffice to give the truth conditions of what we *thought* to be quantification in the object language (which might of course be our own language minus the truth predicate). Perhaps now it will be said that this criticism of a theory of truth based on sub-quantification (as we may now call it) assumes Convention T as a criterion of a truth theory. I agree; it does. There is no simpler or more radical test, and our discussion of sub-quantification is just one more way of bringing this out.

Quantificational structure makes trouble for semantic theory because it allows predicates of any degree of complexity to build from a finite stock of simple predicates, connectives, variables, and quantifiers (or whatever you want to call the devices that do their work in natural language). This blocks the obvious strategy of defining truth for a complex sentence on the basis of the truth of its parts: the parts may not be sentences and hence capable of truth. Sub-quantification tried to bypass the difficulty, but without the kind of success we looked for.

Tarski set the problem (in essence), and he also showed a way to solve it. His solution requires us first to characterize a relation called *satisfaction*, in terms of which truth may be defined. The entities that are satisfied are sentences both opened and closed; the entities that do the satisfying are sequences of the objects that constitute the subject matter of the language for which truth is being explained—the entities to which its singular terms refer, and over which its quantifiers range. For the sake of a brief and informal sketch of the idea, let me ignore singular terms, and the relativization of the concept of satisfaction to a speaker and a time. Think of the variables of quantification as arbitrarily numbered: then a sequence can be considered as a way of matching the variables of the language with the entities over which the variables range. A sequence satisfies a predicate if the predicate is true of the entities with which its (free) variables are matched; for example, the open sentence gotten by writing first the nth variable and then "is wise" is satisfied by a sequence whose n^{th} member is wise. The recursive characterization of satisfaction must have a clause like this for every basic predicate (which is why they must be finite in number). Connectives are handled as one expects; for example, an alternation of two sentences p and q (which may be open or closed) is satisfied by a sequence if that sequence satisfies p or it satisfies q; and so on. Finally, an existential (universal) quantification of a sentence (open or closed) with respect to the nth variable is satisfied by a sequence just in case that sequence, or some (and every) other that differs from it only with respect to the nth member, satisfies it. Whether or not a sequence satisfies a sentence depends only on what entities it matches with the free variables, so if a sentence is closed, it is either satisfied by all sequences or by none. As is clear from the clauses in the theory for existential and universal quantification, the true sentences are satisfied by all sequences, and the false by none.

If a *correspondence theory* is any theory that characterizes truth by appeal to a relation between language and something extra-linguistic, then a theory based on the concept of satisfaction is a correspondence theory. It seems to me that a number of philosophers who have discussed Tarski's approach to truth have missed this point, often because they mistook the role assigned to T-sentences in a semantic theory, and so failed to appreciate the importance of the notion of satisfaction. It bears repeating, then, that T-sentences serve merely to *test* the theory, but they do not themselves hint of a relation between language and something in the world. Ontology comes in only with satisfaction, and satisfaction is an essential part of the machinery needed to run a recursive theory of truth that satisfies Convention T.

Theories of truth based on satisfaction, and those based on the strategy of facts, are both correspondence theories. And they have this further similarity: just as all true sentences in a Tarski-type theory are satisfied by the same sequences (namely all of them), so, if I am right, all true sentences in a fact-theory correspond to the same fact (or the facts, as in "corresponds to the facts"). But here the resemblance ends. The entities that satisfy sentences are arbitrary orderings of the ordinary objects to which singular terms refer and over which variables (similarly ordered) range—or, as we may alternatively think of them, arbitrary ways of pairing the objects that are the subject matter of the language with the variables of the language. Facts, on the other hand, aim to reflect the semantic structure of the entire sentence, and so in particular what is brought to the sentence by its predicates. I argued that facts flub the job because in the attempt to reflect the whole sentence all facts collapse into one; but the contrast with sequences remains. The contrast comes out best in relation to open sentences—sentences with free variables. Facts correspond to closed sentences only, and this is why, or so I have tried to show, they cannot lead to a satisfactory account of quantification. Sequences, however, satisfy open as well as closed sentences, and satisfaction of closed sentences (and hence truth) is explained in terms of the satisfaction of sentences both open and closed. Different sequences satisfy different open sentences, and since closed sentences are constructed from open, truth is reached, in the semantic approach, by different routes for different sentences. All true sentences end up in the same place, but there are different stories about how they got there; a semantic theory of truth tells the story for a particular sentence by running through the steps of the recursive account of satisfaction appropriate to the sentence. The story constitutes the proof of a T-sentence. (The story, not the T-sentence, is what "gives the meaning.")

A theory of truth based on satisfaction is so instructive about the structure of individual sentences because although it is a kind of correspondence theory, the entities which correspond to (i.e. satisfy) sentences do not themselves reflect the structure. Relative simplicity in the objects is offset by the trouble it takes to explain the relation between them and the sentences they satisfy, for every truth-relevant feature of every sentence must be taken into account in characterizing satisfaction. The payoff is clear: in explaining truth in terms of satisfaction, all the conceptual resources of the language in relation to its ontology are brought to bear.

In this lecture I have tried to connect two things: the idea of an adequate theory of truth and meaning on the one hand, and a concern with what exists on the other. The main result, which seems to me by no means obvious, is that a theory that meets the minimal and transparent test for entailing all T-sentences—sentences of the form " 'Snow is white' is true if[f] snow is white"—such a theory must be a correspondence theory, and call for the existence of entities of certain kinds. What forces the issue can also be specified: it is taking *generality* seriously. There is no accounting for the contribution of quantificational structure to truth except in Tarski's way, at least if one wants to have a theory that goes deep enough to satisfy Convention T.

Lecture III
Quotation (May 20, 1970)

A theory of meaning falls short of providing the most revealing account of the relation between words, speakers, and the world—falls short in ways that I have tried to specify quite sharply—if it does not satisfy Tarski's Convention T, which requires the theory to entail, for each sentence, a theorem stating the conditions under which the sentence is true.[1] As a criterion of theories, Convention T cuts much deeper than would be expected from its simple innocent face. In the course of satisfying it, a theory must reveal the ontology of a language, assign a semantically significant structure to the language as a whole, and a logical form to every sentence.

Convention T is thus a standard against which to measure theories and proposed analyses of various bits of language. It is a stern master, for it invites us to explain, within the constraints we have accepted, all the workings of our language. This is far more than I know how to do, but in the present, and my next two lectures, I will try to give some examples showing what it is like to view various problems about language through this particular filter.

I begin with what may seem a tiny and special case, quotation. I think it will turn out to be a more difficult, and more interesting, subject than has usually been thought.

Quotation is a linguistic device used to refer to typographical or phonetic shapes by exhibiting samples, i.e. inscriptions or utterances, that have those shapes. This characterization is purposely broad and unavoidably vague: broad enough, I hope, to include not only written quotation marks, and spoken phrases like "and I quote," but also the finger-dance quotes often used by philosophers condemned to read aloud what they have written; and vague enough, I suspect, to leave open the question whether the words that began this sentence ("This characterization") are a form of quotation.

In quotation not only does language turn on itself, but it does so word by word and expression by expression, or so it seems, and this reflexive twist is inseparable from the convenience and universal applicability of the device.

---

[1] This paper was written in the course of research supported by the National Science Foundation.

The Structure of Truth: The 1970 John Locke Lectures. Cameron Domenico Kirk-Giannini and Ernie Lepore, Oxford University Press (2020). © Cameron Domenico Kirk-Giannini and Ernie Lepore.
DOI: 10.1093/oso/9780198842491.001.0001

Here we already have enough to draw the interest of the philosopher of language; but one perceives as well connections with further areas of concern such as sentences about propositional attitudes, explicit performatives, and picture theories of reference. If the problems raised by quotation appear trivial by comparison, we may welcome finding an easy entrance to the labyrinth. The going will be hard enough.

When I was initiated into the mysteries of logic and semantics, quotation was usually introduced as a somewhat shady device, and the introduction was accompanied by a stern sermon on the sin of confusing the use and mention of expressions. The connection between quotation on the one hand and the use-mention distinction on the other is obvious, for an expression that would be used if one of its tokens appeared in a normal context is mentioned if one of its tokens appears in quotation marks (or some similar contrivance for quotation). The invitation to sin is perhaps accounted for by the ease with which quotation marks may be overlooked or omitted. But the strictures on quotation often sound a darker note. Thus Tarski, in his famous essay "The Concept of Truth in Formalized Languages," examines the possibilities for an articulate theory of quotation marks, and decides that the only possibilities lead to absurdities, ambiguities, and contradiction.[2] Quine wrote in *Mathematical Logic*, "Scrupulous use of quotation marks is the main practical measure against confusing objects with their names," but then he adds that quotation

> has a certain anomalous feature which calls for special caution: from the standpoint of logical analysis each whole quotation must be regarded as a single word or sign, whose parts count for no more than serifs or syllables. A quotation is not a *description*, but a *hieroglyph*; it designates its object not by describing it in terms of other objects, but by picturing it. The meaning of the whole does not depend upon the meanings of the constituent words.[3]

And Church, while praising Frege for his careful use of quotation to avoid equivocation, himself eschews quotation as "misleading," "awkward in practice…and open to some unfortunate abuses and misunderstandings."[4]

---

[2] Alfred Tarski, "The Concept of Truth in Formalized Languages," *Logic, Semantics, Metamathematics*, Oxford, 1956, pp. 159–62.

[3] W. V. Quine, *Mathematical Logic*, Harvard, 1940, §4.

[4] Alonzo Church, *Introduction to Mathematical Logic*, Volume 1, Princeton, 1956, §8.

There is more than a hint, then, that there is something obscure or confused about quotation. But of course this can't be right; there is nothing wrong with the device itself: it is our theories about how it works that are inadequate or confused.

It is often said that in quotation, the quoted expressions are mentioned and not used. The first half of this slogan is relatively clear sailing. It is the second part, which says quoted expressions aren't used, that seems suspicious. Why isn't incorporation into quotation one use of an expression? Perhaps a first response would be that of course there is *some* sense in which the quoted material is used, but its use in quotation is unrelated to its *meaning* in the language; so the quoted material is not used as a piece of language.

This response may not quite still our doubts. For one thing, there are the troublesome cases where it is convenient both to use and to mention the same expression by speaking or inscribing a single token of the expression. I once resolved to adopt a consistent way of using quotation in my professional writing. My plan was to use single quotation marks when I wanted to refer to the expression a token of which was within, but double quotation marks when I wanted to use the expression in its usual meaning while at the same time indicating that the word was odd or special ("scare quotes"). I blush to admit that I struggled with this absurd and unworkable formula for a couple of years before it dawned on me that the second category contained the seeds of its own destruction. Consider, for example, a passage earlier in this paper where I say, nearly enough:

Quine says that quotation "has a certain anomalous feature."

Are the quoted words used or mentioned? Obviously mentioned, since the words are Quine's own, and I want to mark the fact; this is direct discourse, not indirect. But equally obvious is the fact that the words are used; if they were not, what follows the word "quotation" would be a singular term, and this it cannot be if my remark is to be grammatical. Nor is it easy to rephrase my words so as to resolve the difficulty. For example, it is not enough to write, "Quine used the words 'has a certain anomalous feature' of quotation" for this leaves out what he meant by those words.

Here is another mixed case of use and mention that is not easy to sort out:

Dhaulagiri is adjacent to Anapurna, the mountain whose conquest Maurice Herzog described in his book of the same name.

The last phrase "the same name" cannot mean the same name as the mountain, for the mountain has many names. Rather it means the same name of the mountain as the one used earlier in the sentence. I would say this is a genuine case of quotation, for the sentence refers to an expression by exhibiting a token of that expression; but it is a case that manages without quotation marks.

[Or consider this case:]

The rules of *Clouting* and *Dragoff* apply, in that order.

Temporarily setting aside these last examples as pathological and perhaps curable, there is a way, now standard, of giving support to the idea that in quotation the quoted material is not used. This is the interpretation of quotation proposed by Tarski as the only one he can defend. According to it, a quotation, consisting of an expression flanked by quotation marks, is like a single word, and is to be regarded as logically simple. The letters and spaces in the quoted material are viewed as accidents in the spelling of a longer word and hence as meaningless in isolation. A quotation-mark name is thus, according to Tarski, like the proper name of a man.[5] I shall call this the *proper-name* theory of quotation. Church attributes the same idea to Frege or at least a method with the same consequences. Church writes:

> Frege introduced the device of systematically indicating autonomy by quotation marks, and in his later publications (though not in the *Begriffsschrift*) words and symbols used autonomously are enclosed in single quotation marks in all cases. This has the effect that a word enclosed in single quotation marks is to be treated as a different word from that without the quotation marks—as if the quotation marks were two additional letters in the spelling of the word—and equivocacy is thus removed by providing two different words to correspond to the different meanings.[6]

I quote this passage at length because it demonstrates how, on this topic, even Church may nod. For of course if the quotation-mark name is truly a *new* name, which is the main thrust of the idea, then we cannot say that the old *name* (as contrasted with its letters) even appears in quotation, much less that it is *used* autonomously.

---

[5] Tarski, "The Concept of Truth in Formalized Languages," p. 159.
[6] Church, *Introduction to Mathematical Logic*, pp. 61–2.

Quine has repeatedly and colorfully promoted the idea of the quotation as unstructured singular term. Not only is there his denial, already cited, that quotations are descriptions, but the claim that the letters inside the quotation marks in a quotation occur there "merely as a fragment of a longer name which contains, beside this fragment, the two quotation marks."[7]

The merit in this approach to quotation is the emphasis it puts on the fact that the reference of a quotation cannot be construed as owed in any normal way to the reference (or meaning) of the expressions displayed. But it seems to me that if there is more to the doctrine, that more is false as an account of how quotation works in English (etc.). If quotations are structureless singular terms, then there is no more significance to the *category* of quotation-mark names than to the category of names that begin and end with the letter "a" ("Atlanta," "Alabama," "Alta," "Athena," etc.). On this theory, there is no relation, beyond an accident of spelling, between an expression and the quotation-mark name of that expression. Nothing would be lost, from the point of view of this theory, if for each quotation-mark name we were to substitute an arbitrary and completely unrelated name, for that is what it is for an expression to be a proper name. And so no echo remains, as far as this theory of quotation goes, of the informal rules governing quotation that seem so clear: if you want to form a quotation-mark name of an expression, flank that expression with quotation marks; and, a quotation-mark name refers to "its interior" (as Quine puts it). Nothing left, either, of the intuitively attractive notion that a quotation somehow "pictures" what it is about.

These objections are plenty in themselves to throw doubt on Tarski's claim that this interpretation of quotation is "the most natural one and completely in accordance with the customary way of using quotation marks."[8] But there is a further, and, I think, absolutely decisive objection, which is that on this theory we cannot give a coherent account of the conditions under which an arbitrary sentence containing a quotation is true. To give such an account requires (I have been urging) that we see how to construct for the sentences of the language containing quotations a characterization of a truth predicate "s is true" (properly relativized to a language, or a speaker and a time) such that it entails all sentences of the form

s is true iff p

[7] W. V. Quine, *From a Logical Point of View*, Harvard, 1953, p. 140. Compare *Methods of Logic*, Henry Holt and Co., 1950, p. 38; *Word and Object*, M.I.T, 1960, p. 143; Benson Mates, *[Elementary Logic]*, Oxford, 1965, p. 24.
[8] Tarski, "The Concept of Truth in Formalized Languages," p. 160.

where "s" is replaced by a standardized description of a sentence, and "p" is replaced by the described sentence (or a sentence alike in truth value in the metalanguage). To give such a characterization along the lines first sketched by Tarski is the least we should demand of a theory of meaning for the part of the language under scrutiny; short of this we cannot claim to have shown how the meaning of a sentence depends upon its structure (roughly, its vocabulary and grammar).

We have no guarantee we have uncovered relevant structure in giving a theory of truth unless we succeed in characterizing truth (or satisfaction) using no further semantical concepts; in particular, we cannot rest content with an unanalyzed concept of naming or referring. But then there is no way to satisfy Tarski's demands on a theory of truth but by identifying a finite basic vocabulary and a finite number of truth-affecting methods of composing or transforming the elements into more complex structures, ultimately sentences. Put the other way around, every one of the infinite number of sentences must be construed by the theory as owing its truth or falsity to how it is built from a finite stock of parts by repeated application of a finite number of modes of combination. There are, of course, an infinite number of quotation-mark names, since every expression has its own quotation-mark name, and there are an infinite number of expressions. But on the theory of quotation we are considering, quotation-mark names have no significant structure. It follows that a theory of truth could not be made to cover generally sentences containing quotations. Clearly we must reject the proper-name interpretation of quotation if we want anything like a theory of meaning for sentences containing quotations.

I turn now to a quite different theory of quotation, which may be called the *picture theory* of quotation. According to this view, it is not the entire quotation, i.e. expression named plus quotation marks, that refers to the expression, but rather the expression itself. The role of the quotation marks is to indicate how we are to take the expression within: the quotation marks constitute a linguistic environment within which expressions do something special. This was perhaps the view of Reichenbach, who said that quotation marks "transform a sign into a name of that sign."[9] Quine also suggests this idea when he writes that a quotation "designates its object…by picturing it,"[10] for of course it is only the interior of a quotation that could be said to

---

[9] Reichenbach, *Elements of Symbolic Logic*, Macmillan, 1947, p. 335. Reichenbach says other things that seem to contradict this.

[10] Quine, *Mathematical Logic*, §4.

be like the expression referred to (the quotation marks would spoil the picture—they are the frame). And Church also, in the passage already discussed, toys with the notion that on Frege's theory "a word enclosed in single quotation marks is to be treated as a different word" in that it is used "autonymously," that is, to name itself.

It should be allowed at once that all three of the authors just mentioned, in the very passages alluded to, seem to vacillate between the proper-name theory of quotation and the picture theory. Yet the theories are clearly distinct: and bearing in mind the deficiencies of the proper-name theory, we ought to consider the picture theory on its own. At first sight it promises two advantages: first, it attributes *some* structure to quotations, since it treats them as composed of quotation marks (which set the scene for interpreting their contents) and the quoted material. And, second, it hints, in its appeal to the relation of picturing, of a theory that will draw on our intuitive understanding of how quotation works.

These seeming advantages fade when exposed to the light. The difficulty is this. What is wanted is an explanation of how quotation lets us refer to expressions by picturing them. But on the present theory, quotation marks create a context in which expressions refer to themselves. So how does picturing feature? If an expression inside quotation marks refers to itself, the fact that it *also* pictures itself is simply a diverting irrelevancy.

Would it help to say that quotation marks create a context in which we are to view the contents as a picture of what is referred to? Not at all; this is merely a tendentious way of saying the expression refers to itself. In brief, once the content of the quotation is assigned a standardized linguistic role, the fact that it happens to resemble something has no more interest for semantics than onomatopoeia or the fact that the word "polysyllabic" is polysyllabic.

Another important point might escape us here. The picturing relation as between an object and itself is hardly interesting, and the theory, as we are interpreting it, tries vainly to make something of this drab idea. But the more interesting picturing we sense in quotation is not at all between expression and expression. In quotation, what allows us to refer to a certain expression, which we may take to be an abstract shape, is the fact that we have before us on the page or in the air something that *exhibits* or *has* that shape—a token, written or spoken.

The picture theory so far suggests no way at all to bring an inscription or utterance into the picture. This could be done only by describing, naming, or pointing out the relevant *token*, and no machinery for this purpose has been introduced.

Before I leave this stage of the discussion, I would like to mention Frege again. The picture theory of quotation is reminiscent of Frege's theory of opaque (what he called oblique) contexts such as those created by "necessarily," "Jones believes that...," "Galileo said that...," and so on. There are conspicuous differences between these contexts as analyzed by Frege and quotation as treated by the picture theory: in quotation words may change their part of speech (everything becomes a name or description), while in the other contexts this never happens; and in quotation, but not in other opaque contexts, nonsense makes sense. But there is the striking similarity that in both cases some linguistic device is supposed to create a context within which words play new referential roles. This concept of a context that alters reference has never been properly explained, and Frege himself was leery of it: it certainly does not lend itself to direct treatment in a theory of truth. I think there is a way to make sense of the idea; but it will take us some distance beyond anything in Frege.

It may help illuminate the situation to substitute for the picture theory of quotation another theory that contains no mysteries but is similar in some respects. (This theory is purely heuristic; it is not even potentially a theory of how quotation works in English.) A trouble with the picture theory, as with Frege's treatment of opaque contexts generally, is that the references attributed to words or expressions in their special contexts are not functions of their references in ordinary contexts, and so the special context-creating expressions (like quotation marks or the words "said that") cannot be viewed as functional expressions.[11] But things do work the other way around; in particular, what words refer to (or otherwise mean), is a function of what they are said, on the theory, to refer to when quoted, namely themselves. So here is the new theory. Regard every word as always and only a name of itself, and any string of words as a description of the concatenation of named expressions. View quotation marks simply as the identity function. Thus quotations name just what habit expects, and they have a standard semantic structure. Finally, interpret the *absence* of quotation marks as a functional expression mapping expressions onto what they name. Thus an unquoted name names what the name function maps that name onto. The only unquoted expressions that will have an independent meaning will be names, but Frege taught us how to take sentences as names (of truth values), so that is no obstacle.

<hr/>

[11] See my "Theories of Meaning" and "On Saying That." [NB: Davidson's manuscript contains no anchor for footnote 11; we have followed the placement of a similar footnote in the published version of "Quotation," which, however, contains no reference to a publication named "Theories of Meaning."]

This theory is the best yet, but it is no better than a simpler one to appear presently; and both are flawed. The only independent merit of the present suggestion is the queer, and hence instructive, light it puts on the picture theory of quotation, and on Frege's theory of reference-influencing contexts. A central defect of the proper-name theory of quotation was that while conceiving quotations as well-formed expressions of the language, it failed to provide an articulate theory showing how each of the infinitude of such expressions owed its reference to its structure. The experiment just concluded showed that it is possible to treat quotations as having semantically significant structure. Let us press on in this direction.

Geach has long insisted that quotations are really *descriptions*, and hence have structure, and he complains of the proper name theory as I have (though he does not connect his complaints with the need for a theory of truth).[12] His theory, as I understand it, is this. A single word in quotation marks names itself; this is a new item of vocabulary, and is not semantically complex (I am not sure whether Geach says this last). So far, the theory is like the proper-name theory. But a longer expression when quoted is a structured description. Thus "Alice swooned" abbreviates " 'Alice'⌢'swooned'," which reads "the expression got by writing 'Alice' followed by 'swooned'." This theory has the advantages of the preceding Fregean theory, and is far simpler and more natural. (It may be called the *spelling* theory of quotation.)

Both Tarski and Quine imply, by things they say, that they see the possibility of a similar theory. Thus Tarski remarks that if we accept the name theory, then quotation-mark names can be eliminated and replaced everywhere by structural-descriptive names,[13] while Quine contends that we can dispel the opacity of quotation, when we please, by resorting to spelling.[14] The device both have in mind is like Geach's except that Geach takes the smallest units to be *words*, while Tarski and Quine take them to be individual *letters* and *symbols*. The result, in the abbreviations of ordinary quotation, is the same. In primitive notation, which reveals all structure to the eye, Geach has an easier time writing (for only each word needs quotation marks) but a harder time learning or describing the language (he has a much larger primitive vocabulary).

There is no difficulty about extending a truth definition to the devices of spelling suggested by Quine, Tarski, and Geach; yet these devices can be

[12] Peter Geach, *Mental Acts: Their Content and Their Objects*, Routlege and Kegan Paul, 1957; Geach, "Quantification Theory and the Problem of Identifying Objects of Reference," *Acta Philosophia Fennica*, 16, 1963, pp. 41–52.
[13] Tarski, "The Concept of Truth in Formalized Languages," p. 160.
[14] Quine, *Word and Object*, p. 212.

thought of as merely abbreviated by ordinary quotation. This claim of mere abbreviation may be backed by describing a mechanical method for going back and forth between the two styles of notation. Thus given the quotation-mark name "Alice swooned," the machine starts at the left by reproducing the first quotation marks, then the letter "A," then another set of quotation marks, then a sign for concatenation, then another set of quotation marks, and so on until it reaches a set of quotation marks in the original. It reproduces these and stops. The result will be:

"A"∩"l"∩"i"∩"c"∩"e"∩"space"∩"s"∩"w"∩"o"∩"o"∩"n"∩"e"∩"d"

Since the two notations are mechanically interchangeable, there is no reason not to consider a semantics for one a semantics for the other: so this *could* be regarded as a theory of how quotation works in English (modifications would work for other languages). But would it be a correct theory of ordinary quotation? There are several reasons for saying it would not. (This is no criticism of Quine, who never put it forward as a theory of ordinary quotation.)

Notice first that the appearance of quotation marks in the expanded notation is adventitious; in most versions of formal syntax they are not used. The theory works by identifying a finite set of units (words or letters) from which every expression in the language to be described is composed. Then unstructured proper names of these units are introduced, along with a notation for concatenation. Such a theory works as well, and is less misleading, if quotation marks are dropped entirely and new names of the building blocks are introduced. To illustrate (following Geach's method), suppose the word "Alice" is named by the word "alc" and the word "swooned" by the word "sw"; then "Alice swooned" would be described by:

alc∩sw
(or using Quine's method)
Ay∩ell∩eye∩see∩ee∩space∩es∩double-you∩oh∩oh∩en[∩ee∩]dee.

This tiny exercise is meant to emphasize the fact that nothing of the idea of quotation *marks* is captured by this theory—nothing of the idea that one can form the name of an arbitrary expression by enclosing it in quotation marks. On the *spelling theory*, no articulate item in the vocabulary corresponds to quotation marks, and so the theory cannot reflect a rule for their use.

The machine simply knows by heart the name of each smallest expression. Clearly, one essential element in the idea that quotations picture what they are about has been lost.

A striking way to see what is and what is not relevant to structure is to try applying existential generalization and substitution of identity. A standard way of demonstrating that quotation as normally used does not wear its structure on its surface is to observe that from

"'Alice swooned' is a sentence"

we cannot infer:

($\exists$x) ("x swooned" is a sentence)

or:

($\exists$x) ("Alice x" is a sentence)

nor, supposing "alc'" names "Alice," can we infer:

"alc swooned" is a sentence

nor:

alc "swooned" is a sentence.

But (using Geach's version of the spelling theory) we can go from:

"Alice swooned" is a sentence

to:

"Alice"$^\cap$"swooned" is a sentence

and thence to:

alc$^\cap$"swooned" is a sentence

and then to:

($\exists$x) (alc$^\cap$x is a sentence)

or:

($\exists$x) (x$^\cap$"swooned" is a sentence)

In Quine's version of the theory, we could go from:

"Alice" is a word

to:

"A"$^\cap$"l"$^\cap$"i"$^\cap$"c"$^\cap$"e" is a word

to:

($\exists$x) ($\exists$y) x$^\cap$"l"$^\cap$"i"$^\cap$y$^\cap$"e" is a word.

These derivations show clearly that quotation marks play no vital role in the spelling theory; and also that this theory is not a theory of how quotation works in natural languages.

One essential element of picturing has been lost, but not perhaps quite all, for the spelling theory does appear to depend on the description of complex expressions reproducing the *order* of the expressions described. In the description provided by the theory, names of particular expressions need not resemble what they name, but in the description as a whole, names of expressions that are concatenated are themselves concatenated.

Even this residue of the picturing idea is superficial, however. The descriptions the spelling theory provides are themselves, from the point of view of a fully articulate language, mere abbreviations of something more complicated in which the order of expressions may well be changed. (We have suppressed parentheses, the description operator, the elimination of descriptions if necessary, etc.) I think we should conclude that the spelling theory of quotation has no connection with the view that we understand quotation as picturing expressions.

There are further important uses of quotation in a natural language that cannot be explained by the spelling theory and could not be accommodated by a language constructed in the way it suggests. The spelling theory cannot, at least in any obvious way, deal with those mixed cases of use and mention we discussed earlier, nor indeed with any case that seems to depend on a demonstrative reference to an utterance or inscription. An important use for quotation in natural language is to introduce new notation by displaying it between quotation marks; this is impossible on the spelling theory provided the new notation is not composed of elements that have names. On the spelling theory we also could not use quotation to teach a foreign language based on a new alphabet or notation, for example Khmer or Chinese. Since these are functions easily performed by ordinary quotation (whether or not with quotation marks), we cannot accept the spelling theory as giving an adequate account of quotation in natural language.

We have discovered a short list of conditions to be satisfied by a competent theory of quotation. The first is that like a theory for any aspect of a language it should merge with a general theory of truth for the sentences of the language. The other conditions are specific to quotation. One is that the theory provide an articulate semantic role for the *devices* of quotation (quotation marks, or verbal equivalents). When we learn to understand quotation we learn a rule with endless applications: if you want to refer to an expression, you may do it by putting quotation marks around a token of the expression you want to mention. A satisfactory theory must somehow embody or explain this piece of lore. And finally, a satisfactory theory must explain the sense in which a quotation *pictures* what is referred to, otherwise it will be inadequate to account for important uses of quotation, for example to introduce novel pieces of notation and new alphabets.

It is not hard to produce a satisfactory theory once the requirements are clear. The main difficulty springs, perhaps it is now obvious, from the simultaneous demands that we assign articulate structure to quotations and that they picture what they mention. For articulate linguistic structure here must be that of description, and describing seems to forestall the need to picture. The call for structure is derived from the underlying demand for a theory of meaning, here thought of as a theory of truth; all that is needed is enough structure to implement the recursive characterization of a truth predicate. Still, enough structure will be too much as long as we regard the quoted material as part of the semantically significant syntax of a sentence. The cure is therefore to give up this assumption.

It is natural to assume that words that appear between the boundaries of a sentence are legitimate parts of the sentence; and in the case of quotations, we have agreed that the words within quotation marks help us to refer to those words. Yet what I propose is that those words within quotation marks are not, from a semantical point of view, part of the sentence at all. It is in fact confusing to speak of them as words. What appears in quotation marks is an *inscription*, not a shape, and what we need it for is to help refer to its shape. But on my theory, which we may call the *demonstrative theory* of quotation, the inscription inside does not refer to anything at all, nor is it part of any expression that does. Rather it is the quotation marks that do all the referring, and they help refer to a shape by pointing out something that has it. On the demonstrative theory, neither the quotation as a whole (quotes plus filling) nor the filling alone is, except by accident, a singular term. The singular term is the quotation marks, which may be read "the expression a token of which is here." Or, to bring out the way in which picturing may now be said genuinely to be involved: "the expression with the shape here pictured."

It does not discredit this theory to say that it neglects the fact that the quoted material is *syntactically* part of the sentence; taken in abstraction from semantics, the question of location is trivial. In spoken sentences, temporal sequence plays the role of linear arrangement in writing. But if I say, "I caught a fish this big" or "I caught this fish today," my hands, or the fish, do not become part of the language. We would easily enough remove the quoted material from the heart of the sentence. Quotation is a device for pointing to inscriptions (or utterances) and can easily be used, and often is, for pointing to inscriptions or utterances spatially or temporally outside the quoting sentence. So if I follow a remark of yours with "Truer words were never spoken," I refer to an expression, but I do it by way of indicating an embodiment of those words in an utterance. Quotation marks could be warped so as to remove the quoted material from a sentence in which they play no semantic role: we could write:

⤳Alice swooned.⤶ The expression with
this shape is a sentence.

I take it to be obvious that the demonstrative theory assigns a structure to sentences containing quotations that can be handled in a straightforward way by a theory of truth—assuming of course that there is a way of accommodating demonstratives at all. On this point, I have already tried to indicate why there is not any real difficulty in making room for demonstrative or indexical elements in a formal theory of truth.[15] And I hope it is also obvious that the picturing feature of quotation has been exploited and explained. So the demonstrative theory also authorizes the use of quotation

---

[15] Davidson, "Truth and Meaning," *Synthese*, 17, 1967, pp. 304–23.

in introducing new bits of typography and discussing languages with new alphabets. I shall conclude by considering how it fares with the mixed cases of use and mention on exhibit earlier.

I said that for the demonstrative theory the quoted material was no part, semantically, of the quoting sentence. But this was stronger than necessary or desirable. The device of pointing can be used on whatever is in range of the pointer, and there is no reason why an inscription in active use can't be ostended in the process of mentioning an expression. I have already indicated an important sort of case, and there are many more. ("You pay attention to what I'm going to say," "Why did you use those words?" etc.) Any token may serve as target for the arrows of quotation, so in particular a quoting sentence may after all by chance contain a token with the shape needed for the purposes of quotation. Such tokens then do double duty, once as meaningful cogs in the machine of the sentence, once as semantically neutral objects with a useful form.

Thus:

Quine says that quotation "has a certain anomalous feature"

may be rendered more explicitly:

Quine says, using words with this shape, that quotation has a certain anomalous feature. ↲

And as for Anapurna,

Dhaulighiri is adjacent to Anapurna, the mountain whose conquest Maurice Herzog described in his book with a name of this shape.

[Finally:]

The rules of *Clouting* and *Dragoff* apply, in the order in which these tokens appear.[16]

[16] The *Clouting* and *Dragoff* example comes from John Ross. [Ross, "Metalinguistic Anaphora," *Linguistic Inquiry*, 1(2), 1970, p. 273.]

Lecture IV
Attributions of Attitude
(May 22, 1970)

When we try to give a systematic account of what makes our statements true (when they are), the problems that surface often show a common pattern. One scenario that soon becomes familiar is this; in the first act, it is noticed that there is a difficulty in the theory we had been taking for granted. We may have assumed that some word or phrase was a singular term, but then we became aware that this assumption leads to absurdities. In the second act we attempt the obvious cure: treat the offending word or phrase as syncategorematic—as a meaningless part of a larger meaningful whole. That larger whole is then considered a semantic primitive, a unit without structure significant to theory. (An expression is a semantic primitive relative to a theory if the rules for the sentences in which it does not occur do not suffice for the sentences in which it does occur. The theory must take independent account of it.) In the third act, it turns out that if this course is systematically pursued, there must be an infinite number of primitive expressions; and this means no satisfactory theory is possible.

Our study of quotations illustrates the pattern. In a state of prelapsarian innocence we suppose that quoted expressions are semantically part of the sentences in which they feature, and are the parts of speech they seem. This proto-theory leads to trouble, made manifest when we try to quantify into quotation from outside. Next comes the syncategorematic response (of Tarski and Quine): deny relevant structure, and treat quotation marks and enclosed material as proper names. The curtain falls as the hero (quotation marks) and heroine (quoted material) realize that this much oneness will not be tolerated by convention (Convention T, which in effect bars a theory that treats an infinity of expressions as primitive).

When it works, there is every reason to push for syncategorematicity, for when it works it just amounts to removing redundant structure, and with it, very often unwanted intimations of ontology. The ontologist bent on economy may wield his frightening razor, but the same effect is accomplished in semantics by merely exempting longer and longer sequences of

The Structure of Truth: The 1970 John Locke Lectures. Cameron Domenico Kirk-Giannini and Ernie Lepore,
Oxford University Press (2020). © Cameron Domenico Kirk-Giannini and Ernie Lepore.
DOI: 10.1093/oso/9780198842491.001.0001

words from the effects of theory. It is the healing process of mending up the wounds between words left by semantically insignificant spelling accidents. In exploring the limits of syncategorematicity, we are learning what entities we cannot get along without.

[What is the structure of "Socrates is wise," and what its ontology? One answer that has often been suggested is that "Socrates" and "wise" are names, the first of Socrates and the second of, say, the property of wisdom. The "is" then expresses the relation of exemplification. But unless we feel compelled to quantify into the position occupied by "wise," there is nothing to prevent us from welding the "is" and the "wise" into a single unstructured predicate (let us suppose, anyway: in fact many reasons might prompt us to find structure here). The same cannot be done for "Socrates" as long as we want to preserve some natural connection between "Socrates is wise," "Someone is wise," and "Everyone is wise." For once we decide to treat the position occupied by "Socrates" as one that can be occupied by variables of quantification (or pronouns that act in essentially the same way), we know that no adequate theory can fail to treat that position, and whatever comes to occupy it, as a separate bit of structure, and one that has ontological significance.

It might be thought that the issue still has not been forced, since the truth conditions for each of a finite number of sentences like "Socrates is wise" (with one or another proper name for Socrates) could be given by enumerating the cases, and the same could be done for the quantifications of each simple predicate. All this could be done, and the relation between "Socrates is wise" and "Everyone is wise" explained, without any necessity for explaining this relation as involving *replacement* of a variable by a name (or vice versa). And so without having to identify the predicate "is wise" as a *common* element, an essential bit of structure.

What forces the issue is the possibility of building up predicates of any degree of complexity. There are an infinite number of predicates, given a finite vocabulary, and the resources of quantification and connectives. This prevents us from enumerating the cases, and forces a recursive account. It is the recursion that in the end imposes structure. One lesson is this: the deep asymmetry between subject and predicate comes out only when we study a sentence in the setting of the whole language.]

I turn now to the problem of providing an acceptable semantic analysis of sentences used to describe what is said, believed, intended, asserted, or commanded—in short, what are often called sentences about propositional attitudes. At least some attributions of attitude can be put into the form of:

description of agent—verb (perhaps followed by "that")—sentence, and it is these only that I shall discuss.

We will have a semantics for belief sentences and their troublesome kin when we see how to extend a theory of truth to cover them. This gives the project a well-defined goal, but it should be pointed out that it has not been the goal, or the only one anyway, of many philosophers who have worked in this area. The semantic problem has often been identified with the apparent failure of substitutivity of identity—the fact that although the author of *Waverly* and the author of *Ivanhoe* were one, someone may believe that Scott is the author of *Waverly* without believing that Scott is the author of *Ivanhoe*. This particular puzzle might be resolved, it has often been pointed out, by treating "the author of *Waverly*" and "the author of *Ivanhoe*" as descriptions, and analyzing descriptions along the lines first proposed by Russell. But the move does not provide a general theory of truth; at best it removes one obstacle to providing one. It remains a problem that someone may believe Nixon to be a featherless biped but not a rational animal.

The example shows that giving a truth definition raises a more general problem about attributions of attitudes than is always raised, or answered. But giving a truth definition falls short in other ways of being all that has been sought. Philosophers have often wanted, in addition to a viable semantics, a reductive analysis of belief. When Carnap proposed in *Meaning and Necessity* that a sentence of the form "John believes that snow is white" be analyzed "John is disposed to an affirmative response to some sentence in some language that is synonymous with 'Snow is white'," he was partly doing semantics and partly trying to analyze the concept of belief in behavioristic terms. The two projects are related, of course, but I think there are excellent reasons for keeping the distinction clearly in mind. One is that we are apt to reject a theory that is semantically unexceptionable because we do not like the philosophy that went with it; another is that we may be tempted to accept a piece of semantics that works only for what we fancy to be an improved model of our mother tongue. The fruits of this comparison are particularly apparent in the analysis of intentional idioms, for here those who have had a theory have usually also held that natural language needs neating up if it is to serve the purposes of science, or even high-grade rational discourse.

My interest is science too, but the science of natural language. It would defeat this purpose to improve the object: what wants improving is not our language, but our theory of it. No doubt plenty of simplification will go on: to get ahead with the job, we will have to idealize the object of study. But this is a compromise to put up with until we can do better, and should not be represented as an exercise in conceptual slum-clearance.

Let us work on *assertion* as our sample propositional attitude. The familiar pattern at once emerges. The naive theory must be that in the content sentence (as I shall call it) that follows the name-asserted-that formula all is as it appears to be: the singular terms and predicates that constitute the content sentence have their normal references and roles. There follows the trouble for truth that Frege pointed out so carefully. The next scene in the skit is supposed to introduce a theory that treats a normally articulate stretch of sentence as syncategorematic.

There is no dearth of theories to carry the plot forward. The most extreme is Quine's, made, perhaps, not quite seriously, in *Word and Object.* There Quine proposes that we consider the words that follow the name or description of an agent in an attribution of assertion to be a semantically unstructured one-place predicate. (This gives my picture of the situation; Quine certainly does not describe it so. He ascribes structure, using concepts drawn from syntax, and provides no semantics. From the point of view of a theory of truth, one must, I think, count this as assigning no semantical structure.) This approach, it should be clear, solves the problem of substitution in assertion sentences only by entirely thwarting theory. There can be no theory of truth of the kind we have been discussing for Quine's proposal, because it entails an infinity of unstructured, hence primitive, predicates. "... asserts that everything flows" is one such predicate. It is easy to appreciate how many more such predicates there are.

Israel [Scheffler] has suggested instead an infinity of unstructured (from a semantical point of view) predicates of utterances. So he would analyze "Heraclitus asserted that everything flows" as "There exists an utterance x such that Heraclitus asserted x and x is a that-everything-flows utterance." This overcomes various objections to other proposals, but is intractable semantically, as is any theory that treats as syncategorematic a passage of a kind that has an infinite number of variants.

To be classed with [Scheffler]'s proposals are a number of more recent theories. It is natural, in response to discovering that the naive theory fails, to reason this way. The words that follow "asserts that" do not behave as usual because they merely serve to characterize an assertion. Their function is therefore essentially *adverbial.* "Heraclitus asserted that everything flows" really means no more than that Heraclitus made an assertion—that he performed a certain speech act—and he did it in a certain manner. The manner was the everything-flows manner. This suggestion is, in a way, the worst yet, for it saddles us, first of all, with an infinity of unanalyzed adverbs, and then asks us to assume we understand the semantics of adverbial modification. But in fact, adverbial modification itself is an unsolved problem for a straightforward theory of truth, as I shall try to show in my next lecture. For the moment it is enough to observe that calling the content sentence, in attributions of attitude, adverbial solves the basic problem only by obliterating it. It does not substitute a good theory for a bad one; it substitutes a theory-thwarting proposal for a bad theory.

It is a little harder to see that Church's idea of a language that can handle assertion sentences cleaves to the usual pattern. Taking a cue from Frege, Church suggests that after the occurrence of "asserts that," expressions should be introduced that denote intentional entities. For example, instead of writing "Pamela asserted that Smith kissed her" we should replace "Smith" with a word that denotes the usual sense or intention of "Smith," say "Smith" with a subscript, "$Smith_1$." If the assertion locution is iterated, Smith goes up a level: thus "Pamela asserted that $Smith_1$ kissed her" yields "Smith asserted that $Pamela_1$ asserted that $Smith_2$ kissed her." (I'm ignoring what happens to the predicates.) These name-plus-subscript-expressions cannot be regarded as semantically complex, for no semantic operation answers to the syntactical operation of adding a subscript to a name. The explanation is simply that the sense of an expression is not a function of its extension. And now it is easy to detect the familiar difficulty. Since "asserted that" can in principle be iterated indefinitely, any subscript to a denoting expression can be pushed a step higher than an arbitrarily chosen finite subscript. But an old expression with a new subscript is simply a new expression semantically: Church's language contains an infinite number of semantic primitives. It cannot be a prototype for a natural language, if a natural language can be described by a finite theory of meaning.

Frege deplored the fact, as he saw it, that in natural languages the same expression can have an unlimited number of references (and senses), and perhaps he would have viewed Church's modification (adding subscripts) as an improvement. In fact there is little on the basis of which to choose. Frege suggested the following rule for determining the reference of an expression. Compute what might be called the semantic level of an expression by counting the number of verbs of attitude that dominate it. If the level is zero, the expression refers to (and here we need a rule giving the "ordinary" reference); if the level is n, the expression refers to the sense of the same expression when it has level n−1. Here the context does the work (roughly) of Church's subscripts; and the results are much the same for theory. Expression plus context cannot be regarded as semantically complex; the result is that an expression with level n must be treated as a new primitive relative to that expression with any lower level. There is no top level, so there cannot be a finite theory. Once more syncategorematicity has been pushed beyond what theory can tolerate, though this time syncategorematicity has a form one might not notice: what has been welded into a single unit semantically is an expression plus an index gotten by counting the number of occurrences of verbs of attitude that dominate it.

Not every analysis of assertion sentences that posits intensional entities (propositions, properties, senses, individual concepts, etc.) leads to unworkable infinities of unstructured expressions, or the equivalent (as in Frege). Matters can be patched up various ways so far as the difficulties we have just canvassed are concerned. If, for example, we were to decide that prefixing an assertion sentence with another verb of attitude (and appropriate subject) did not alter the conditions of substitution in the inmost content sentence, then the semantic levels could be held down to two. (Carnap suggested essentially this in *Meaning and Necessity*, and later, and in a more strictly Fregean context, Michael Dummett.) And given this limitation, they can be attractively interpreted as having only one semantic level by introducing a *reality-function* mapping senses onto references. Such a theory has expressions all of the same level referring, some of them, to intensions, and others, always complex, to extensions. To see how it might work for a simple case: imagine that the predicate "is wise" stands for a function that maps people onto truth values and *also* (a further reach of its domain) individual concepts onto propositions. A name like "Socrates" names an individual concept. So if we want to talk of the man Socrates, we need to talk of the entity onto which the reality function maps the concept referred to by "Socrates." So our English sentence "Socrates is wise" is given this new form: "The reality of Socrates is wise." The sentence "Socrates is wise," on the other hand, strictly names a proposition. We can, then, get back to truth with "The reality of (Socrates is wise)"—the same entity (the True) as is named by "The reality of (Socrates) is wise." "Plato believed that Socrates is wise" on the other hand becomes "The reality of (Plato) believed that Socrates is wise." The important point here is the *absence* of the reality operator in front of "Socrates."

This exercise is perhaps a help if only because by contrasting it with Frege's actual theory we grasp better how that theory falls short of total application of Frege's own basic principle of building the sense and reference of a sentence on the repeated application of function to argument. By applying this principle in the case of attributions of attitude, we get a semantics that yields to theory in the sense of satisfying Tarski's Convention T.

The language with which we have just been toying requires an ontology of abstract entities—intentions or one sort and another—but it is a purely extensional language. Substitutivity of identicals is straightforward, and works as well for content sentences as elsewhere. I point this out to separate issues: although, as we saw, many theories that appeal to intensional entities obstruct a theory of truth, not all do.

There are other reasons, however, for rejecting any such theories as final. Given more time it would be good to argue the matter in detail; as it is, I shall vent my misgivings only briefly before moving on to my own analysis of assertion sentences (and other sentences used to attribute attitudes). This analysis will serve in part as a comment on the limitations of other theories, for it will be obvious that the virtues I find in my proposal cannot be shared by theories that depend in the usual way on propositions or other intensional entities.

I have been urging the claim of a T-theory—a theory of truth that satisfies Tarski's Convention T (modified to apply to a language with indexical elements)—to be the core and substance of a theory of meaning. The theme is in part to show how little we have explained of the workings of language without such a theory, and in part to show how surprisingly much a theory of this kind does explain. The second theme is muted to the degree that the theory employs powerful concepts that it does not elucidate. So a theory that can state the truth conditions of "Heraclitus asserted that everything flows" only by appeal to an ontology of persons and things that flow is vastly superior to a theory that requires persons (at least one) and propositions (or other intensional entities), for whatever additional entities the first theory required (the flowing things) will be needed by the second theory to analyze "Everything flows." The first theory is superior not because it gets along with *fewer* entities (though this is true) but because it gets along without entities that are mainly characterized by properties designed (or defined) to solve the problem. This does not mean a theory that appeals to propositions or intensions has no explanatory power, only that it obviously has less than theories that do without—assuming, of course, that the same appearances are saved.

[Much of what is attractive about Convention T as a criterion of a radical theory of truth and meaning is that it requires a theory that throws up, for each sentence *s* in the language under study, a statement giving the truth conditions of *s*, while using conceptual resources essentially identical with (and hence no stronger than) the resources of *s* itself. A theory that must refer to propositions in giving the truth conditions of a sentence like "Heraclitus asserted that everything flows" may or may not sin against the letter of this criterion—that depends on some delicate technical matters and some tricky decisions about conceptual resources—but it does, I think, sin against the spirit of the criterion.]

So far my point is only that a theory that invokes intensional entities to account for the truth of attributions of attitude explains less than theories that do without—a safe enough contention. Now I should like to hint why I think such theories are wrong. It will help to begin by saying I find no fault with the view that a person expresses a certain proposition (or makes a statement) when he speaks, or, more generally, that the objects of the propositional attitudes are propositions. These views are not necessarily semantical in character, and the worst that I would say about them is that they postulate entities that serve no useful explanatory purpose. What I object to is the idea that recognizing propositions is any direct help in interpreting assertion sentences (etc.). The reason it isn't is brought out as follows: it is the difference between *expressing* a particular proposition and *naming* or *describing* it. What proposition I express may depend—must depend, I would say, if there are propositions—on factors that far outrun the rules of language. But what my words describe or refer to must be fixed by the rules. The word "I" in my language refers to the speaker, quite independent of context. No explanation can alter this except by altering the language. But if I say, "Jones asserted that Agnew is soft on communism," explanation may well be called for to get the attribution right, and this is not because the words are obscure. It is because "that Agnew is soft on communism" does not name an entity. The explanation is appropriate because—to put it a way I don't much like—I have *expressed* a proposition by the words "Agnew is soft on communism," but I haven't named it. And what I expressed, or wanted to express, since it outruns questions of meaning in the sense in which meanings are fixed by the conventions of language, can bear endless explaining. You know what my *words* mean, but not necessarily what *I* mean, when I say, "Jones asserted that Agnew is soft on communism." I take this to prove that the words "that Agnew is soft on communism" do not *name* a proposition.

The distinction I am after between what a speaker's words mean when uttered and what (in addition) a speaker may succeed in expressing by those words featured in my delimitation of the role of theory in the study of meaning (it is concerned only with what the words mean, though this is a concept relativized to occasions of speech). That distinction now appears again in the analysis of attributions of attitude, for if I am right, many philosophers have mistakenly inferred, from the fact that I can convey the contents of another man's speech, belief, desire, or intention by using a sentence of my own that expresses the same content, that the point of my sentence must have been to name or describe the shared content. I have just urged that this inference is a mistake.

Before I develop these remarks into a theory, I want very briefly to mention analyses of sentences about propositional attitudes that use model theory—or possible worlds, if that is different—in one way or another. It is fairly obvious that such analyses suffer from the same limitations as theories that directly introduce meanings or propositions. Though the constructions are more ingenious, and so often provide a far more impressive fit with the workings of natural language, they do not explain meaning and reference in terms of something more basic, but by freely fashioning complex abstract entities designed for no other purpose than to fit the pieces together they echo the patterns of inference we think, or know, we are committed to. I do not say these projects are not of value; if nothing else, they emphasize the difficulties a better theory must overcome. But I do suggest that they fail to explain, in any deep sense, how, by using language in the ways we do, we convey truths about the attitudes of others.

The feeling that model-theoretic versions of truth do not carry us as far as T-theories is reinforced by the discovery that a model-theoretic semantics does not yield the theorems required by Convention T. Truth, to put it briefly and crudely, is defined in terms of truth in a model, and this feature, which is entirely lacking in the simple theories that satisfy Convention T, stops us from accounting for the truth conditions of each sentence using only concepts drawn from that sentence.

*   *   *

Every theory we have considered is based on the following reasoning. Premise: in assertion sentences and other sentences of attitude-attribution, extensionalism breaks down; in particular, the substitutivity of identity appears to fail. Conclusion: the words of the content sentence (or what does its work in grammatical variants) cannot be performing their normal semantic functions. The solutions differ widely, but all are solutions to the problem *as just formulated*. Syncategorematic theories treat as semantically unstructured sequences that are normally structured; Fregean theories introduce whole universes of strange entities to serve as extensions for familiar words; possible-world-model-theoretic approaches alter the semantics of expressions in content sentences by more complex methods, but alter them they do.

I think we should reject the reasoning on which these theories are based. The premise is clearly true: normal substitutions based on coreference fail when applied to sentences about attitudes. The conclusion, however, does not follow: it does not follow that the semantics of the content sentence are different from the semantics of the same sentence when it stands alone. *Something* is different; that's a cinch. But there is no reason why it should be the semantics, in the narrow sense of semantics that restricts it to questions of meaning, reference, and truth as determined by the conventions of the language—the narrow sense that alone can be encompassed by a theory.

The conclusion that philosophers have learned to accept, that the rules of reference and truth change radically when a sentence is embedded in a belief- or assertion sentence, seems to me in itself wildly improbable. Suppose I say, "The moon constitutes a severe threat to our security. This was asserted yesterday by the Mayor of the Indian Ocean." The second remark certainly affects how a hearer reacts to the first, what he takes the speaker to have been up to, what he takes the speaker to have meant or intended in saying what he did. But how can the second remark alter the *linguistic* rules that apply to the first, how can it alter what the expression "the moon" refers to, or the truth value of the whole? Of course, the second remark can alter our *interest* in whether, in making the first remark, I spoke the truth; but anything might do that.

Let me try to bring out the idea by altering the example slightly. First I say, "The moon constitutes a severe threat to our security." Then I add, "I understand that you say this too." Here it is natural to recognize the first remark as serving two purposes: first, it is made in my own behalf, perhaps assertively. Second, it enables me to convey the content of something you say too. These two tasks are carried out, not by my first speaking the words assertively and then by my referring back to the words and assigning them a new use. Rather it is the first speaking of the words I need to refer back to. My remark, " 'I understand that you say this too" is true if and only if we are *coasserters*, and this we are if, in saying "The moon constitutes a severe threat to our security," I asserted something you assert. So that remark serves two purposes, as it happens, but so far as those two purposes are concerned, my *words* cannot have two interpretations. What the words meant when I spoke them determined what I asserted, and that assertion is all that is needed, on my side, to verify my claim that we are coasserters.

There is so far no problem for semantics. Assuming our theory of truth can cope with sentences like "The moon constitutes a threat to our security" (and let's not worry about *that*!), then no further problem arises about

"You assert that too." The "that" is a demonstrative, perhaps with a tacit sortal modifier "remark" or "utterance," referring to my own last remark. Spelled out a bit, "You assert that too" means roughly "Some assertive remark of yours in the past, and my most recent assertive remark, made us coasserters." The reason the standard semantical problems don't arise is that the words of my first remark are not semantically part of my second remark. *Any* change in the words of this first remark, even substitution of coreferring singular terms (as "largest satellite of the earth" for "the moon"), changes the reference of the demonstrative in the second remark, and so *may* change it from true to false.

With some fairly obvious refinement I think this analysis will serve for sentences—or rather utterances—about attitudes generally. First I shall concentrate on the relation of coassertion which holds between speech acts. My main point about this relation has already been made, that it is not analyzable solely in terms of linguistic rules. This is not only because it involves the concept of assertion, which is not (I have argued) a matter of linguistic convention. Coassertion is not reducible either to synonymy of sentences assertively uttered. The reason is not that the meaning of a sentence relative to a speaker and a time cannot be captured, but rather that what is captured is not strong enough, unless relativized to a scheme of translation arbitrarily chosen, to yield a usefully strong sense of synonymy as between speakers. What is arbitrary so far as the rules of language are concerned need not be absolutely arbitrary, and the success of attributions of attitude depends on this. Two utterances are coassertions because of what the words of two speakers, as uttered, mean—but because, also, the contexts of utterance settle more than the rules of language can.

Although the relation of coassertion cannot be analyzed in terms of linguistic meaning, we *can* abstract from it these separable elements, that of assertion, and that of sameness of content. The two speech acts are synonymous in the strong sense discussed; *and* they are both assertive. Since these elements are separable, we can define a new relation as follows: it holds between two speech acts when they are synonymous, and the first is assertive. This is the relation that holds between some past utterance of yours and my present utterance of "The moon constitutes a threat to our security" if my words "You asserted that" are true in the following context: "You asserted that. The moon constitutes a threat to our security." To spell this out a bit, I'll expand the first sentence: "Some past speech act of yours was an assertive utterance synonymous with my next utterance (which may or may not be assertive). The moon constitutes a threat to our security."

Indirect discourse can be analyzed along the same lines. "Heraclitus said that everything flows" has the logical form of two sentences. The first sentence, "Heraclitus said that," consists of a two-place predicate flanked by a name and a demonstrative, the demonstrative referring, or purporting to refer, to an utterance. The utterance was made in this case by my saying "Everything flows." The first sentence was true if an act of saying of Heraclitus' was synonymous with my saying; if we were *samesayers*.

Belief does not require a speech on the part of the believer. Attributions of belief, desire, intention, hope, and so on, in so far as they can be put into the form of name—verb (that)—sentence, therefore express a relation between a person and an utterance of the attribute[r]. So if I say, "Thales believed that there is a god in the magnet," what I say may be analyzed (that is, its semantics may be sketched) as here: "The following remark gives the content of a belief of Thales. There is a god in the magnet." We could connect belief more directly with the language of the believer: "If Thales had honestly expressed his belief, his remark would have been synonymous with mine to follow. There is a god in the magnet."

I would like to take a few minutes to connect the present paratactic analysis of attributions of attitude with my earlier analysis of quotation. It has often been suggested that in attributions of attitude, the content sentence should he treated as quoted material—of course this is a way to shortcut problems about substitutivity of identity. Given the usual theory of quotation—that quotations are unstructured names—this could hardly be paraded as a solution; at best it would reduce the problem of sentences about attitude to the problem of quotation. But suppose this difficulty overcome (perhaps by treating quotations as structured descriptions); there remains a more subtle objection. The objection is that even a sentence relativized to a time and person does not pick out a meaning accurately enough to serve for an attribution of attitude *unless the sentence is actually used by the person at that time*. A theory of the language can say what, so far as the conventions are concerned, it is for a sentence to be true for a person at a time whether or not he speaks. But I have been urging that this is not enough—an actual utterance will, and must, convey more. Suppose, then, that I am allowed only to *refer to* (and not *to use*) the content sentence in an assertion sentence: "Heraclitus asserted that everything flows" becomes something like: "Heraclitus uttered assertively a sentence that meant in his mouth then what 'Everything flows' *would* mean in my mouth now were I to *speak* it and not merely *mention* it." But in the strong sense of meaning involved, what *would* these words mean in my mouth now? Who can tell, since the circumstances that are relevant are just those that I control by the context of utterance?

On the theory of quotation that I suggested in my last lecture, however, it is possible both to use *and* to mention a sentence. So the analysis of "Heraclitus asserted that everything flows" could be "Heraclitus uttered assertively a sentence that meant in his mouth then what the sentence, a token of which will appear next, *does* mean in my mouth now. Everything flows." This analysis is more complicated than necessary, but it is essentially equivalent to the one we had already reached. Clearly the demonstrative and paratactic approach to attribution of attitude may be viewed as using quotation if quotation is construed demonstratively.

Most attempts at systematic theory encounter a problem when it comes to first-person attributions of attitude. It seems to me, therefore, to reinforce the demonstrative paratactic analysis that it leads to a very natural solution of the puzzle. The puzzle is this. If I say, or even assert, that Galileo asserted that the earth moves, I don't necessarily, or perhaps ever, myself assert that the earth moves. How then can it happen that if I utter the following sentence assertively I *do* assert that the earth moves? Here is the sentence:

I assert that the earth moves.

I would say that it is obvious that if this sentence is true (now, for me), then I do assert that the earth moves. But this only deepens the mystery, which is, how (on earth!) did I do it? The puzzle arises because on most theories speaking the words "the earth moves" in the context created by the words "Galileo asserted that" *cannot* constitute an assertion. And yet we recognize that in saying "I assert that the earth moves" I may very well assert that the earth moves. A similar problem arises, of course, for "I promise that...," "I command that...," "I question whether...," and other such locutions. What most theories cannot explain is how it is *possible* to assert that p by saying "I assert that p." We should not make the mistake of asking for an explanation of why someone who truthfully says "I assert that p" *necessarily*, in so saying, asserts that p, for he may not. For suppose first that I assert that p. Then I say playfully, and not at all seriously, "I assert that p." Then this second remark is *true*, but I did not assert that p in saying it.

To appreciate how the problem is solved by the paratactic analysis, let me dwell on certain aspects of the proposal. The utterance of a sentence like "Galileo asserted that the earth moves" is, according to me, to be analyzed as the performance of two speech acts, one after the other, each with its semantically complete and independent expression (in all but punctuation a sentence). The first act, which we may call the *prologue*, sets the scene for the second, which we may call the *play*. It sets it in the sense that it invites us, normally, to take the play as doing no more than conveying the content of some other speech act, or the character of an attitude. The prologue thus usually functions somewhat like the words "Once upon a time"; it defuses the natural implications of the play. The prologue cannot, however, *dictate* the illocutionary character of the play—nothing can do that. And the prologue itself may be spoken playfully—as indeed we are invited explicitly to think when verbs of attitude are iterated. So in "Smith asserted that Jones asserted that p" the "Jones asserted that" is prologue to the utterance of "p," but the play relative to *its* prologue "Smith asserted that."

In the first-person present-tense case, the play may serve two purposes: first, it may, as usual, convey the content of some utterance by being synonymous with it, and second, it may *be* that utterance. This comes about in a straightforward way. I attribute an assertion to Galileo by saying (in effect):

> My next remark is synonymous with a past assertion of Galileo. The earth moves.

I attribute the same assertion to myself by saying:

> My next remark is synonymous with a present assertion of mine. The earth moves.

Here the prologue is true if I do assert that the earth moves, and if the play is an assertion, the prologue is verified. Clearly if the prologue is an assertion too, this is normally in itself a great step toward making the play an assertion. So putting these things together, it is easy to see that first-person present-tense prologues tend to be self-fulfilling: by asserting them, we can hardly help but make them true.

The result we have just reached depended, I hope it is clear, on mechanically applying the general analysis of attributions of attitude to the first-person case. It is often assumed that no ordinary semantic analysis can account for the fact that in saying "I assert that p" or "I promise that p" we very often do assert or promise that p, but I think I have shown that this assumption is wrong.

The truth values of prologue and play vary independently. In third-person attributions, or any that are not first-person present-tense, if we care about truth at all, it is apt to be the truth of the prologue that concerns us. If we ask whether it is true that Heraclitus asserted that everything flows, what we want to know is whether Heraclitus asserted *that*, not whether everything flows. But in the first-person present-tense cases, we know that if truth is at issue, it can't be the prologue we wonder about. On the other hand, if the prologue is true, then the play comes into prominence in its own right, for it *is* an act of assertion, promising, or commanding. So if that act is one that focuses on truth in turn, we will mainly consider, in the first-person attribution (*self*-attribution), whether the play is true.

These remarks underscore the importance of the principle that we must keep distinct the question whether a sentence, on a particular occasion of use, *has* a truth value and what the conditions of its truth are, and whether its truth is at *issue*. The first concerns, as I have been putting it, what the *words* mean; the second, what the *speaker* means. A closely related principle is that the illocutionary force of an utterance cannot be a function merely of what words mean. These two principles combine to suggest that in the analysis of *mood* the question whether a sentence, say in the indicative, interrogative, or imperative, *has* a truth value is of little importance. For mood is surely a matter of meaning, and this is independent of whether the words are used to convey truth, tease it, or question it.

Briefly, there are these two axes along which utterances can vary: the words may be in one or another *mood* (indicative, imperative, interrogative); and the utterance may be in one or another *mode* (assertive, querying, commanding). The first axis concerns linguistic meaning, the second does not. Whether someone speaks the truth is a matter of what his words mean, though whether we raise the issue or even *say* that he spoke the truth may depend on more; but basically, the question whether the sentence one uses has a truth value is simply unrelated to the *mode* of utterance. So most objections to saying that interrogatives or imperatives are true or false are based on a confusion of mood and mode.

To acknowledge that imperatives, say, can be true or false is not to provide any clue to their analysis. Indeed, it begins to look a harder problem than ever, for if the difference, say, between an imperative and an indicative is not to be represented by an "illocutionary force indicator," what can represent it?

If we begin by supposing, as many do, that there is a common core to corresponding indicatives, interrogatives, and imperatives (and others?), and we think of the difference as residing in some kind of sentential operator (as Frege seems to have done), we are faced with a semantic problem that cannot, I think, be solved within the limits we have set. The reason is discouragingly simple: a whole sentence semantically embedded in another has only one semantic attribute we have yet discovered: its truth value. The realization of this is what has led us to paratactic solutions of quotation and sentences about propositional attitudes, for these methods remove sentences that seem embedded in others from their beds.

I suggest the same approach to moods. Not that moods should be directly reduced to first-person present-tense attributions of attitude. "Close the door" does not mean what "I command that you close the door" does. The latter mentions me as commander in a way the first certainly does not; but also the second mentions *commanding* in a way the first does not. These differences are easily caught by a paratactic analysis, however. "I command you to shut the door" is, in my analysis, "My next remark conveys the content of a command of mine. You will close the door." This allows a natural variation over commanders and times, which is essential to the analysis of "x commands that p." But "Close the door" should be rendered by something like "The next remark is imperative in mode. You will close the door." Here the prologue allows no room for variation over people or times, and makes no reference to command. Rather it *refers* to the mode of utterance, whether truly or not. Of course, speaking the prologue in the right way is apt to make the play a command; but again, this is a matter that goes far beyond what linguistic convention can determine.

Lecture V
Adverbial Modification (May 27, 1970)

A theory of truth that satisfies Tarski's convention T works best—without complication or compromise—when applied to a language that can be viewed as consisting of just these elements: a finite number of predicates (each with some fixed number of places); a denumerably large number of variables along with the existential and universal quantifiers; and connectives, truth-functional in nature, connecting sentences both open and closed. (I assume that these devices carry with them whatever punctuation, if any, is required.)

In this list there are really only two sorts of iterative device: the compounding of sentences (open or closed) to form sentences, and the application of quantifiers to sentences. The definition of truth (or satisfaction) must parallel these devices in the clauses of its recursion. In so doing it cannot fail to foist elementary quantification theory on the object language, in the sense that if a sentence S entails a sentence T according to quantification theory, then it will be possible to prove, from the theory of truth alone, that if sentence S is true, sentence T is also true. The sign for identity in the object language, like the sign for class membership, is, from the point of view of truth theory, just one more two-place predicate, not to be distinguished in kind from "is to the left of" or the transitive "adores." The *logic* of identity, on the other hand, in the form of substitutivity of identity and the rest, creeps into the object language by way of the definition of satisfaction for quantifiers, and certain obvious assumptions about sequences (for example, that for every sequence assigning a certain entity to a given variable of the object language, there must be another sequence that assigns a *different* entity to that variable, and *identical* entities to all other variables).

Proper names, even if finite in number, raise new problems because of the threat of non-reference, while definite descriptions (if the description operator is unreduced) raise this problem, and more. Description is a new *recursive* device, and demands a new recursion in semantics to go with it—a characterization of the relation of *denoting*.

Aside from complications about non-referring singular terms—and this is a subject I am deliberately avoiding—descriptions raise no problems that

The Structure of Truth: The 1970 John Locke Lectures. Cameron Domenico Kirk-Giannini and Ernie Lepore, Oxford University Press (2020). © Cameron Domenico Kirk-Giannini and Ernie Lepore.
DOI: 10.1093/oso/9780198842491.001.0001

cannot be met by a T-theory (as I have been calling a theory of truth satisfying Convention T). By modifying Convention T in a natural way, we have already seen our way clear to accommodating indexical features of a language and, by exploiting various opportunities this left open, we were able to suggest techniques for treating quotations, attributions of attitude, performatives, and moods within an extensional first-order language. A further modification might allow us to cope with non-referring singular terms and sentences neither true nor false.

A language with all this—a language for which we know to give a T-theory—is powerful enough for most of mathematics and much of science; perhaps all we need. Still, the aim is not a theory of meaning merely for the language of science, but a theory for a full-blooded natural language; and from this point of view the devices at hand may seem weak and wrong. Let me, all too briefly, indicate why I am sanguine of success.

First, the basic pattern of quantification theory is what we *know* how to accommodate in a T-theory; it does not follow that other patterns are not possible. Convention T is our sole criterion of success in spinning a theory, and it does not mention any particular constraints on the nature of the recursive devices a language can contain. Quantificational structure may not be rich enough to serve as a model for English, but perhaps there are other sorts of structure that will serve, and for which we can give a theory of truth.

Second, it must come as a surprise to many philosophers that a number of linguists, on one or another of the many moving fronts of transformational theory, have recently been coming to the view that quantificational structure may serve as a guide to the deep structure of English. These linguists, led on by the problem of devising a satisfactory generative syntax rather than by the urgings of logicians and philosophers, have been discovering the advantages of treating pronouns on the lines of variables, of abolishing the distinctions between common nouns, verbs, and adjectives in deep structure, of giving basic sentences the form of predicates with places for singular terms or variables rather than the subject-predicate form, and so on. Two further and recent developments that please me because they are parallel with ideas that I have proposed independently, and for different reasons, are the notion that every sentence of English must be represented in deep structure as introduced by a semantically separate mood-setter; and the idea that verbs of change and action require an ontology of events.

These signs of unexpected rapprochement between linguistics and logic may or may not show that in the end deep structure and logical form must be treated as identical. I think they must if linguistics is to be serious about semantics; but someone who disagrees may at least grant this: the whole development of linguistics touched off by Chomsky shows that there is no practical chance of accounting for the surface structure of a natural language without postulating underlying structures that are *very* different—far simpler in the total number of devices on which they call, and vastly more complex, generally, than the particular surface structures they support. It seems to me that merely by acknowledging this we disarm any easy criticism of the thesis that quantificational structure is adequate to the semantics of natural language.

My third reason for optimism is, I am afraid, a typical philosopher's reason, and one I might deplore in another. I think we *can* give a T-theory of truth for English (or any language) because there *must be* one. Each of us knows, in the way such a theory requires, what it is for an arbitrary sentence of his language to be true. And since our powers are finite, this knowledge must boil down to something finite, and something that does not exceed the conceptual resources of the language. A theory of truth that satisfies Convention T shows how, in a finite length of time, it is possible to teach someone who knows English a theory of truth for the whole of English. One is then able to spell out every detail of the conditions on the concept of truth or satisfaction using only his (and one's own) original, and non-semantic, vocabulary. When the account is finished, a new concept will have been explained, though of course *it* cannot be part of the language that has been explained. It seems to me that only a theory with the characteristics I have just mentioned shows how a language *could* be learned from scratch.

These remarks can hardly be expected to persuade skeptics; all that will persuade them, I imagine, is the *fait accompli*. Let me turn, then, to a family of problems we have so far barely noticed. In the last lecture I suggested how the scant resources of a theory of truth satisfying Convention T might be made to cope with sentences in which the substitutivity of identity breaks down; or, as I would put it, what look to be sentences in which the substitutivity of identity appears to break down.

Curiously enough, there are problems set for a straightforward semantics by the fact that in certain contexts, coreferring singular terms *can* be substituted *salva veritate*. A simple example concerns expressions of temporal priority. "The chairman's resignation preceded the fall of the government" makes no obvious trouble because it seems to have the form of two singular terms—"The chairman's resignation" and "the fall of the government"— flanking a relational predicate, "preceded." To accept this analysis is, of course, to accept an ontology of events—it is to suppose that "the chairman's resignation" refers to an entity in the same way that "John" does in "John smote Jack." I think the supposition is true, and that we should accept the analysis; but clearly before we can be happy about it, terms like "The chairman's resignation" must be related to sentences like "The chairman resigned." If "The chairman's resignation" refers to an event, "The chairman resigned" must imply that an event occurred; yet nothing in its surface grammar suggests reference to an event.

It might be thought that we can escape taking events this seriously by reflecting that "The chairman's resignation preceded the fall of the government" seems simply a rearrangement of the elements of "The chairman resigned before the government fell," and here nothing in the grammar suggests names or descriptions of events; the ostensible ontology consists of nothing but the chairman and the government. Why not just say the truth conditions (and so the ontology required) for "The chairman's resignation preceded the fall of the government" are the same as for "The chairman resigned before the government fell"?

There are two difficulties with this proposal. The first is that the two sentences do not have the same truth conditions. The reason is that the description "The chairman's resignation" implies, or presupposes, that the chairman resigned exactly once within the assumed scope of reference—it purports to pick out a particular resignation, while there is no such implication or presupposition in the case of "The chairman resigned." If the chairman first resigned, then the government fell, then the chairman was reinstated, and then he again resigned, it would remain true that he resigned before the government fell—this is consistent with his also resigning after the government fell. But given this same story, we could not simply say the chairman's resignation preceded the fall of the government.

The second difficulty is that "The chairman resigned before the government fell" does not have an obvious semantic structure. Clearly, substitutivity of identity works for "The chairman" and "the government." But if we accept the principle of substitutivity, and the principle that logically equivalent sentences can be substituted for one another without affecting the truth of the whole, then we have all it takes to set Frege's argument in motion that proves we have a wholly extensional context—in particular, a truth-functional context. Yet "before" is not a truth-functional sentential connective. It is like "and" (which is truth-functional) in that a before-sentence cannot be true unless both component sentences are. But that is not enough; for a true before-sentence is turned false by reversing its components. There is, then, a clash between treating "before" and "after" as sentential connectives, and finding a semantic analysis that satisfies Convention T.

We owe the central idea of this analysis of the problem to Frege, though he did not, of course, put it in terms of a theory of truth; and we owe to him also the standard solution. It is an astonishingly ingenious solution, and it proposes a logical form for sentences of temporal priority that is remote from surface grammar. Where we thought there were two closed sentences joined by the connective "before," Frege tutors us to see three open sentences knit together by existentially quantified variables, and two conjunction signs, thus: "There exist two times, t and t' such that the chairman resigned at t, the government fell at t', and t was before t'." Three surprises: "before" comes out a relational predicate; "resigned" and "fell" reveal themselves as having extra relata; and an ontology of *times* emerges to occupy the new places. The inference to "the chairman resigned" is properly implemented. But how about the relation between "the chairman resigned" and "the chairman's resignation"? Let that wait a moment.

Consider sentences that have much in common with sentences of temporal priority: singular causal statements. Here is an example: "The chairman's resignation caused the fall of the government." Once again we have, or seem to have, two singular terms flanking a relational predicate, but variants exist that give other impressions. Here are a few: "The chairman's resigning caused the government to fall," "The government fell because the chairman resigned," or even "The chairman resigned, and that caused it to come about that the government fell." Again we recognize that substitutivity of identity works, that if "caused" (or some of its substitutes) is a sentential connective, it forms a sentence that is true only if, but not necessarily if, the sentences it joins are true.

We are in precisely the same bind we found ourselves in with "before" and "after"; and not very surprisingly the same solution works. Now, however, it is *events* over which we need to quantify, and not times. So the logical form of our sentence must be, "There exist two events, e and e', such that the chairman resigned e, the government fell e', and e caused e'." According to this proposal, "The chairman resigned before the government fell" and "The chairman resigned, which caused the government to fall" have exactly the same logical form, with "caused" replacing "before." The first, it is true, we had introducing times where the second needed events, but this is a difference we would do well to resolve in favor of events, since events, but not times, are related by both causality and priority. As a fringe benefit, we can justify as literal, if not true, Hume's thesis that a cause must precede its effect.

A feature of this analysis of causal sentences is that though it forces us to take events as entities in their own right, it does not interpret a sentence like "The government fell because the chairman resigned" as having expressions that refer to any particular events. What this sentence says, according to the theory, is that there exist two events that fulfill certain conditions—the sentence is existential and general with respect to events. We can simplify the point by considering one of the sentences entailed by "The government fell because the chairman resigned." This has a logical form made apparent as "There exists an event such that the chairman resigned it" or (a little better) "The chairman made a resignation." The only singular term is "the chairman"—"a resignation" is, as usual, an expression whose logical properties we try to catch with an existential quantification.

Now we are in a position to resolve the question how "the chairman's resignation" and "the chairman resigned" are related. The second, as we have just seen, employs a two-place predicate "resign" that is true of resigners and their acts of resignation, and "the chairman resigned" says this predicate is true of the chairman and some act of his. "The chairman's resignation," on the other hand, is a definite description which logicians would render, using a description operator, "The act (event) such that it is a resignation of the chairman." So a sentence employing this phrase, such as "The chairman's resignation caused the fall of the government," imputes, or entails, singularity of events.

Two important matters thus seem to come out as they should: first, a natural relationship is set up between phrases like "The chairman's resignation" and sentences like "The chairman resigned" in which an identical semantic component corresponds to the verb "resigned" and to an aspect of the nominalization. And, second, the sentences "The chairman's resignation caused the fall of the government" and "The chairman resigned, which caused the government to fall" have different truth conditions, since the first, but not the second, imputes singularity of cause and effect.

Because what we are after is a systematic statement of the conditions under which sentences are true, we cannot give (the sentence) "The government fell" one analysis when it is embedded in a causal sentence, or entailed by a causal sentence, and another when it appears alone. Its truth conditions do not change, unless, of course, it is ambiguous. But then we must face the fact that if our analysis is correct, *every* sentence with a verb of change or action is explicitly about events: "Yuichiro Miura skied down Everest" is true only if there is an event of his skiing down Everest; "Juliette ate a cockle" requires at least one cockle and one eating: "The bombing occurred at midnight" entails, or presupposes, that there was one, and only one, relevant bombing, and it occurred at midnight.

I do not think we should hesitate to embrace the conclusion that many of our statements have a logical form that commits us to taking them as referring to, or quantifying over, events. All of the grammatical apparatus of reference in connection with events is present in English, and would in any case have to be accounted for. We speak freely of the identity of events (that time his parachute failed to open was (identical with) his last jump); we use the definite and indefinite articles; there is a rich supply of sortal concepts (sets, games, points, tournaments in tennis; ascents, pitches, rappels, Tyrolean traverses in mountain climbing; clangs of the bell, journeys to London, encounters in the fog, kisses, knocks, landings, and takeoffs); and, to go with these, counting. It is astonishing that philosophical logicians have thought that sentences containing these devices could be systematically represented in quantification theory *without* introducing an ontology of events.

A further consideration that ought to help reconcile us to an ontology of particular or concrete events is that they lead to an acceptable semantics of adverbs and adverbial modification. The problem was discussed in a special form by Anthony Kenny in his book *Action, Emotion and Will*. Kenny emphasized what he called the "variable polyadicity" of verbs of action—the fact that one can apparently add indefinitely to the number of places such verbs have. So we can say "Preston shaved" and then add, in installments (at each stage we have a complete sentence), "with a razor," "in the kitchen," "on Saturday." Standard logical practice calls on us to introduce a new predicate, with one more place to be occupied by a singular term or variable, for each new suffixed clause. But to add a place to a predicate is to create a new predicate, semantically quite independent of the first. There seems no clear end to how many supplementary clauses can be added (particularly if we think of the iterative property of "by" and "in order to" phrases). But then we are forced, by the standard method, to admit in place of each verb, like "shave," a potential infinity of verbs of action, which means we cannot give a satisfactory theory of truth.

Even if it did not lead to an infinite primitive vocabulary, we should be unhappy with the idea that there is no common semantic feature corresponding to the verb "shave" in "Preston shaved" and "Preston shaved with a razor" and all the rest. We should be unhappy not only because it is obviously false, but because we will then have given no semantic foundation for the inference from "Preston shaved with a razor" to "Preston shaved."

The problem Kenny raised is even more persuasive than he noticed, for it afflicts not only talk about action, but all talk of change. ("The tree fell on the house during the winter" entails "The tree fell on the house" and "The tree fell" and "The tree fell during the winter"; not one of these entailments is justified on the basis of logical form in the usual analysis.) The solution we found for causal sentences works here too. If the fall of the tree is an event to which we can refer, we can say as much or as little as we please about it. Even if no particular fall is mentioned, a sentence may say there exists (at least one) fall of a tree, and go on to add further details some such fall had. And so our sentence, analyzed along these lines, comes out with a form we can give thus: "There exists an event such that the tree fell it (i.e. it was a fall of the tree), it was a fall onto the house, and it occurred during the winter." There was clearly a recursive device at work, as evidenced by the menace of an infinite vocabulary; that device is now revealed as the familiar one of quantifier, variable, and conjunction. And as for Preston, there was a shaving by Preston, it was with a razor, it was in the kitchen, and it was on Saturday.

A new difficulty appears with a sentence like "The rock broke the window." "Broke" can also act the part of what seems a one-place predicate, in "The window broke." So far, this is a problem we have conquered. What is new is that following our recent strategy, we will infer "The rock broke" from "The rock broke the window," whereas what we want to infer is "The window broke." I think we can cope with the puzzle with the tools on hand, but only by combining the analysis of causal sentences with the analysis of adverbial modification. We may regard "The rock broke the window by striking it" as a rearrangement of "By striking it the rock broke the window," that is, "A striking of the window by the rock caused a breaking of the window." If we generalize a bit on striking, we can say "A movement of the rock caused a breaking of the window." And this last is, I believe, very close to "The rock broke the window." The expanded sentence, however, has, on the event-analysis, this underlying form: "There exist two events, one a motion of the rock, the other a breaking of the window, and the one caused the other." This entails, by ordinary quantification theory, that there exists a breaking of the window, i.e., that the window broke.

Can we treat "John broke the window" in a parallel way? It would seem so, since surely "John broke the window" means that a motion of John's caused the window to break. But no, this will not in general give the right analysis, and the reason seems of some interest to the philosophy of action.

"John broke the window" covers two very different cases: one, the normal, where John strikes the pane intentionally; and second, the odd, where Jane, we suppose, throws John through the window. It is only this second case that is really parallel with "The stone broke the window." If we want to give the form of the standard case, we must express the fact that John stood in a certain special relation to the movement of his that caused the window to break—a relation we may call that of *agency*. I suggest, then, that we give the form of "John broke the window" along these lines: "There was an event of which John was the agent, and another event that was a breaking of the window, and the first event caused the second."

Another example will illustrate the flexibility of the method, as well as its prolixity. "John broke the window with a rock" should be analyzed as involving three events, the first a movement of which John was the agent, the second, a movement of the rock, and the third, a breaking of the window. The first event caused the second, and the second the third. Given the transitivity of causality, we may infer that John broke the window.

I believe there is a case known to lawyers of a man who stood in Rhode Island and shot a man standing in Massachusetts. It mattered for some reason where the man was tried, and that depended on where the shooting took place. A did shoot B, but where? I cannot help the lawyers, but I think I do see a simple source of the ambiguity. "A shot B" means "There was an event of which A was the agent and an event of B being shot (the shot penetrating his body) and the first event caused the second." If we add "in Massachusetts" to "A shot B" we realize that this clause can give the location of either event, but that in the example it cannot give the location of both. "A shot B in Massachusetts" corresponds to (at least) two semantical structures: "There was an event of which A was the agent, and which was in Massachusetts, and it caused an event of B being shot," *or* "There was an event of which A was the agent, and it caused an event of B being shot, which occurred in Massachusetts."

An interesting problem comes to the fore with sentences such as "The ball rolled to the bush" or "He shot the arrow through the axe heads." The problem is that the first entails "The ball rolled" and the second "He shot the arrow," but we have no natural verb to correspond to the second half of each sentence. "The ball rolled to the bush" can hardly be analyzed in terms of two events and the relation of causality, for what is the second event? "He shot the arrow through the axe heads" should, I think, involve two events, and a causal relation, "He was agent of an event that caused the arrow to be shot through the axe heads," but even if this be accepted, the problem remains encased in the description of the second event; subtract agency, and you still have "The arrow shot (i.e., went like a shot) through the axe heads."

Any adequate theory should show how "The ball rolled to the bush" contains a discreet semantic element corresponding to the verb "roll." This is clear not only because of the valid inference to "The ball rolled" but also because one does not want to treat a long list of expressions that contain the same verb as semantically unrelated—I mean expressions like "rolled into," "rolled through," "rolled beyond," etc. What is wanted, obviously, is a way of handling *prepositions* as semantically independent items. The only satisfactory way I know to do this within a theory of truth is to view prepositions as predicates of events: so the "to" of "The ball rolled to the bush" is a two-place relational predicate true of places or objects on the one hand, and events on the other. The place or object marks the location toward which the event was directed, and at which it terminated. "The ball rolled to the bush" then has this structure: "There was an event that was a rolling of the ball, and that event was a motion towards, and terminating at, the bush." Given this structure, the original sentence can now be seen validly to entail "The ball rolled." It also entails "There was a motion towards, and terminating at, the bush"; this seems to be correct.

In my last lecture I remarked briefly that it could hardly count as *solving* a problem in the analysis of a troublesome kind of statement to call some stretch of words adverbial. The reason I gave was that adverbs posed an unsolved problem in semantics. Now that we have before us a suggestion about how to view some cases of adverbial modification, we can reconsider the prospects for adverbial analysis. The first point to make is obvious. Adverbial analyses are typically *nominalistic* in intent: the idea is to show that one or another kind of entity that seemed to be needed is not. On my view, adverbial clauses are absorbed into predicates, and so have no ontological implications in themselves. But these predicates require various entities for their satisfaction, and in particular I found no way of doing the semantics of many cases of adverbial modification without introducing *more* ontology than seemed at first to be required.

It is a story that I hope is now familiar: it is easy enough to seem to avoid ontological entanglements as long as one accepts no responsibility for an analysis of structure and entailment.

The second point about *some* adverbial analyses is that not even our present methods can touch them. It is sometimes said, for example, that *thinking* should be adverbially analyzed, thus avoiding the need to posit intensional objects of thought. A proposal might be to render "Helen thought the pool was full" as "Helen thought in a that-the-pool-was-full fashion."

Another similar suggestion is that a sentence like "The mountain looked a dirty, sad lavender to him" be given the form, "The mountain appeared to him in a dirty-and-sad-lavenderish-way." These proposals will not yield to the methods I have been exploring because they treat as semantically unstructured expressions that can be grammatically replaced by endless other expressions. Yet each of these expressions must, when placed in that position, be considered unstructured—at least if ontological implications are to be avoided.

Let me say a little about two more very common forms of adverbial modification. One results from the appearance of those troublesome and fascinating adverbs of action like "voluntarily," "inadvertently," "on purpose," "intentionally," "maliciously." These words affect their whole linguistic environment, interfering with the substitution of coreferential terms and coextensive predicates (except for the name or description of the agent). The analysis must therefore revert to the radical methods that apply to attributions of attitude. I see "voluntarily" and its ilk as much on a par, semantically, with "believes," "thinks," and the "says" of indirect discourse. "Cressida carelessly destroyed Troilus" has, then, in part, this form: "It was careless of Cressida that she destroyed Troilus." The verb of carelessness relates Cressida and a speech act of mine that gives the content of her attitude. But of course there is also more: an act of which Cressida was agent caused a destruction of Troilus.

The other form of adverbial modification I have left to last, not because it is unusual—on the contrary—but because I do not know what to say about it. "Salome danced well" certainly entails "Salome danced," but the first sentence cannot mean that there was an event that was Salome's dancing, and it was done well. This won't work because that same action of Salome's falls under other descriptions, and yet under those other descriptions (e.g., "seducing the king") we might or might not want to say the act was done well. "Salome danced well" means her action, *considered as a dancing*, was done well. But it might be considered in other ways. The problem is not due to the evaluative word—the same problem arises for "slowly."

We recognize the pattern of trouble from attributive *adjectives*: "Rudolf is a brawny man" can't mean "Rudolf is brawny and Rudolf is a man" since Rudolf is also a dock worker, but not a particularly brawny one of them. In the case both of attributive adjectives, and what we might as well call attributive adverbs, it is tempting to put the weight on a comparative form.

"Rudolf is brawnier than Clarence" and "Salome danced better than Herodias" do not raise obvious problems for semantics. For "Rudolf is a brawny man," we might then proffer "Rudolf is brawnier than most men," which would be good enough, perhaps, if we had an analysis of the quantifier "most". I will not follow this trail any further since it does not lead to any striking successes.

There is much more that could be said about adverbial modification—I have, as is perhaps all too obvious, merely scratched the surface structure. But I hope I have succeeded in giving color to the idea that quantificational structure, or some other that like it submits to direct semantical analysis, may suffice to represent the logical form of sentences in English. The Procrustean enterprise consists essentially in trying to show that a few of the grammatical resources of English, and ones that may not seem very obvious at that, suffice to explain all of them. From the point of view of semantics, what I would like to demonstrate is that the items of logical structure that closely match the surface of a few idioms constitute, in one arrangement or another, the logical structure of every sentence.

One striking feature of the method is that a large number of grammatical categories come to have representatives that are of the same semantical category. We were prepared for the assimilation, in deep structure, of common nouns, verbs, and adjectives to predicates. In this lecture I have urged that many adverbs, or clauses of adverbial modification, must go the same way. Prepositions also I thought there was reason to provide with the semantics of predicates. Finally, for at least one case—that of agency—there seems to be a good argument for thinking that *case*, which among other things is a means of symbolizing the relation between an entity and an event, can also be represented by a predicate. The effect of carrying this idea to its conclusion would be to fragment event- and action-sentences even further: for example, "Shem kicked Shaun" might become "There was an event that was a kicking; Shem was the agent of the event, and Shaun the patient." I see no objection to this, and it has the merit of making the passive transformation a purely surface phenomenon.

Each of these moves I have described as a way of giving "the logical form" of one kind of sentence or another. It seems to me I ought, in concluding this lecture, to try to give some account of this concept.

One point of assigning a logical form to a sentence is to locate the sentence logically in the totality of sentences: to describe it in a way that explicitly determines what sentences it entails and what sentences it is entailed by. The location must be given relative to a specific deductive theory; so logical form itself is relative to a theory. The relativity does not stop here, either, since even given a theory of deduction there may be more than one total scheme for interpreting the sentences we are interested in that preserves the pattern of entailments. The logical form of a sentence is, then, relative both to a theory of deduction and to some prior determination as to how to render sentences in the language of the theory.

Seen in this light, to call the paraphrase of a sentence into some standard first-order quantificational form *the* logical form of the sentence seems arbitrary indeed. Quantification theory has its celebrated merits, to be sure: it is powerful, simple, consistent, and complete in its way. Not least, there are more or less standard techniques for paraphrasing many sentences of natural languages into quantificational languages, which helps excuse not making the relativity to a theory explicit. Still, the relativity remains.

Since there is no eliminating the relativity of logical form to a background theory, the only way to justify particular claims about logical form is by showing that they fit sentences into a *good* theory, at least a theory better than known alternatives. In so far as I have been calling quantificational form logical form, I was assuming that quantification theory is a good theory. What's so good about it?

Well, we should not sneeze at the virtues mentioned above, its known consistency and completeness (in the sense that all quantificational truths are provable). I have elsewhere criticized Reichenbach's analysis of sentences about events, which introduces an operator that, when prefixed to a sentence, results in a singular term referring to an event. I gave the standard argument to show that on this theory, if one keeps substitutivity of identity and a simple form of extensionality, all events collapse into one, and I concluded that Reichenbach's analysis was radically defective. One might, however, protest that Reichenbach gets in no trouble if the assumption of extensionality is abandoned, and the assumption is mine, not Reichenbach's. This is a fair response; I ought not to have said the analysis was defective, but rather that on a natural assumption there was a calamitous consequence. Without the assumption there is no such consequence; but also no theory. Standard quantification theory plus Reichenbach's theory of event sentences plus substitutivity of identity in the new contexts leads to collapse of all events into one. Reichenbach indirectly commits himself to the principle of substitutivity, so he is apparently committed to giving up standard quantification theory. Since he offers no substitute, it is impossible to evaluate the position.

Another idea which is very often put forward is not to tamper with quantification theory, but simply to add some extra rules to it. If we give the quantificational form of "Jones buttered the toast in the bathroom" as "Buttered$_3$ (Jones, the toast, the bathroom)" and of "Jones buttered the toast" as "Buttered$_2$ (Jones, the toast)," then the inference from the first to the second is no longer a matter of quantificational [logic; but why not interpret this as showing that quantificational form] isn't all there is to logical form, and quantificational logic isn't all of logic? We might be able to give a purely formal (syntactical) rule that would systematize these inferences. I think it is easy to underestimate the difficulties in doing this, particularly if, as I have argued, this approach forces us to admit predicates with indefinitely large numbers of predicate places. I also think one easily slights the difference between simple axioms and new rules of inference (or axiom schemata). But harping on the difficulties, unless they can be proven to be impossibilities, is inconclusive. It will be more instructive to assume that we are presented with a satisfactory deductive system that adds to quantification theory rules adequate to implement the entailments between event sentences of the sort under consideration.

What could then be said in defense of my analysis?

What can be said comes down to this: it explains more, and it explains better. It explains more in the obvious sense of bringing more data under fewer rules. Given my account of the form of sentences about events and actions, certain entailments are a matter of quantificational logic; an account of the kind under consideration requires quantificational logic, and then some. But there is a much deeper difference.

We catch sight of the further difference if we ask ourselves why "Jones buttered the toast in the bathroom" entails "Jones buttered the toast." So far, the rule-proposer's only answer is, because "buttered" and some other verbs (listed or characterized somehow) work that way; and my only answer is, because (given my paraphrases) it follows from the rules of quantification theory. But now suppose we ask, why *should* the rules endorse this inference? Surely it has something to do with the fact that "buttered" turns up in both sentences? There must be a common conceptual element represented by this repeated syntactic feature; we would have a clue to it, and hence a better understanding of the meaning of the two sentences, if we could say what common role "buttered" has in the two sentences. But here it is evident that the new rules, if they were formulated, would be no help. These rules must treat the fact that the word "buttered" turns up in both sentences as an accident: the rule would work as well if unrelated words were used for the two- and for the three-place predicates. In the analysis I have proposed, the word "buttered" is discovered to have a common role in the two sentences: in both cases it is a predicate satisfied by certain ordered triples of agents, things buttered, and events. So now we have the beginnings of a new sort of answer to the question why one of our sentences entails the other: it depends on the fact that the word "buttered" is playing a certain common role in both sentences. By saying exactly what the role is, and what the roles of the other significant features of the sentences are, we will have a deep explanation of why one sentence entails the other, an explanation that draws on a systematic account of how the meaning (i.e., the truth conditions) of each sentence is a function of its structure.

To exhibit an entailment as a matter of quantificational form is to explain it better, then, because we do not need to take the rules of quantificational logic on faith; we can show that they are *valid*, i.e., truth-preserving, by giving an account in terms of their quantificational structure of the conditions under which sentences in quantificational form are true. From such an account (a theory of truth satisfying Convention T) it can be seen that if certain sentences are true, others must be. The rules of quantificational logic are justified when we demonstrate that from truths they can lead only to truths, and that all such entailments do come under the rules.

Plenty of inferences that some might call logical cannot be shown to be valid in any interesting way by appeal to a theory of truth, for example the inference to "*a* is larger than *c*" from "*a* is larger than *b* and *b* is larger than *c*" or to "Henry is not a man" from "Henry is a frog." Clearly a recursive account of truth can ignore these entailments simply by ignoring the logical features of the particular predicates involved. But if I am right, it is not possible to give a coherent theory of truth that applies to sentences about events and that does not validate the adverbial inferences we have been discussing.

Let me state in more detail how I think our sample inference can be shown to be valid. On my view, a theory of truth would entail that "Jones buttered the toast in the bathroom" is true if and only if there exists an event satisfying these two conditions: it is a buttering of the toast by Jones, and it occurred in the bathroom. But if these conditions are satisfied, then there is an event that is a buttering of the toast by Jones, and this is just what must be the case, according to the theory, if "Jones buttered the toast" is true. Someone may still be prompted to ask, "But how does *this* show that 'Jones buttered the toast' is a three-place predicate?" To this I answer that all I *mean* by saying that "Jones buttered the toast" has the logical form of an existentially quantified sentence, and that "buttered" is a three-place predicate, in that a theory of truth meeting Tarski's criteria entails that this sentence is true if and only if there exists...etc. By my lights, we have given the logical form of a sentence when we have given the truth conditions of the sentence in the context of a theory of truth that applies to the language as a whole. Such a theory must identify some finite stock of truth-relevant elements, and explicitly account for the truth conditions of each sentence by how these elements feature in it; so to give the logical form of a sentence is to describe it as composed of the elements the theory isolates.

These remarks will help, I hope, to put talk of "paraphrasing" or "translating" in its place. A theory of truth entails, for each sentence s of the object language, a theorem of the form "s is true if and only if p." Since the sentence that replaces "p" must be true (in the metalanguage) if and only if s is true (in the object language), there is a sense in which the sentence that replaces "p" may be called a translation of s; and if the metalanguage contains the object language, it may be called a paraphrase. (These claims must be modified in important ways in a theory of truth for a natural language.) But it should be emphasized that paraphrase or translation serves no purpose here except that of giving a systematic account of truth conditions. There is no further claim to synonymy, nor interest in regimentation or improvement. A theory of truth gives a point to such concepts as meaning, translation, and logical form; it does not depend on them.

It should now be clear that the only reason for "paraphrasing" event sentences into quantificational form is as a way of indicating the truth conditions for those sentences within a going theory of truth. We have a clear semantics for first-order quantificational languages, and so if we can see how to paraphrase sentences in a natural language into quantificational form, we see how to extend a theory of truth to those sentences. Since the entailments that depend on quantificational form can be completely formalized, it is an easy test of our success in capturing logical form within a theory of truth to see whether our paraphrases articulate the entailments we independently recognize as due to form.

To give the logical form of a sentence is, then, for me, to describe it in terms that bring it within the scope of a satisfactory semantic theory. Merely providing formal rules of inference fails to touch the question of logical form (except by generalizing some of the data a theory must explain); showing how to put sentences into quantificational form, on the other hand, does place them in the context of a semantic theory. The contrast is stark, for it is the contrast between having a theory to back claims about logical form and having no theory, and hence no clear way of making sense of claims about form. But of course this does not show that a theory based on first-order quantificational structure and its semantics is all we need or can have. Many philosophers and logicians who have worked on the problem of event sentences (not to mention modalities, sentences about propositional attitudes, and so on) have come to the conclusion that a richer semantics is required, and can be provided. In analyzing action and event sentences, I have explicitly put to one side several problems that invite appeal to such richer schemes. I think I have shown that the problems isolated can be handled within a fairly austere scheme. But when other problems are also emphasized, it may well be that my simple proposal loses its initial appeal; at least the theory I have put forward in this lecture must be augmented; and perhaps it will have to be abandoned.

Lecture VI
Invariants of Translation
(May 29, 1970)

In the last three lectures, I have considered a number of problems that arise in the course of an attempt to give a satisfactory theory of truth for English. I have tried in particular to establish—or at least render somewhat more plausible—the thesis that even if we limit ourselves to a semantics appropriate to a first-order functional language (a limitation that is not clearly imposed by Convention T), it *may* be possible to extend a theory of truth to handle indexical expressions, quotations, attributions of belief, intention, preference, desire, and the like; performative sentences such as those that begin "I promise that," "I assert that," and so on; moods, singular causal sentences, and adverbial modification in many of its forms.

These problems, and many others to which I did not suggest a solution, arise even when the language under examination, and the language used to frame the theory, are essentially the same. At least in *posing* the problems, there was no need to be self-conscious about the form of T-sentences. Since the object language and metalanguage both were ours, there was generally not much trouble in telling whether a given T-sentence was true, nor in judging whether the resources on which it called were the same, as nearly as possible, as the resources of the sentences whose truth conditions were being given. Perhaps we assumed a bit much; it doesn't matter. For now I wish to turn to the general case, where it cannot be taken for granted that object language and metalanguage are the same, and where, as a consequence, we cannot start off with any assumptions about the relation between the sentence a T-sentence is *about*, and the words the T-sentence provides that state the truth conditions.

In particular, then, we must not suppose that we can tell whether a sentence in our own language (the metalanguage) is synonymous with, has the same meaning as, or is a translation, paraphrase, or canonical representation of, some sentence of the object language. If we cannot tell, independent of having an adequate theory, then we cannot make it a *criterion* of an adequate theory that it entail T-sentences where the truth conditions of a

The Structure of Truth: The 1970 John Locke Lectures. Cameron Domenico Kirk-Giannini and Ernie Lepore,
Oxford University Press (2020). © Cameron Domenico Kirk-Giannini and Ernie Lepore.
DOI: 10.1093/oso/9780198842491.001.0001

sentence *s* (and here by truth conditions I mean just the sentence on the right of the biconditional)—where the truth conditions translate, or are synonymous with, (etc.), *s* itself. Clearly, too, we cannot require that *s* and its truth conditions have the same ontology, or that their singular terms refer to the same things, or that they have the same structure, or that they entail the same things. These are concepts to which the theory must give an application; it cannot require that they be available in advance.

To give a theory of truth for a language that we cannot, or do not, assume to be our own is thus to engage in what Quine calls *radical translation* (though not necessarily to use precisely his methods). And to state criteria for success that are plausibly applicable in practice is to give an account of how communication by the use of language is possible—to give an account of meaning.

The theory is asked to characterize a certain relation between a sentence, a speaker, and a time—a relation such that if it holds at a time when the speaker utters that sentence, then he speaks the truth or, as I urge could equivalently be said, he makes a true statement. The notion of speaking the truth or making a true statement I gave an interpretation that made it independent of any particular illocutionary intentions or accomplishments, and so independent of the notion of assertion. I think this interpretation is one that our use of the phrases "speak the truth" and "make a true statement" allows, for there seems to be no contradiction in this description: "When Sidney coyly said he had no money with him, he did not mean it or believe it; but as it turned out, he spoke the truth." In *this* sense of speaking the truth, I argued, we can give purely linguistic rules that determine whether or not someone who speaks, speaks the truth.

What the rules determine is only whether, *given* that an act is a speech act, it is true; they cannot determine whether it is a speech act. An act is a speech act only if it is done with *some* illocutionary force—it is an assertion, or a command, the issuance of a challenge or an insult, the uttering of a warning, a rebuke, the making of a promise, or the certification of a deed. And so on, through a long, though perhaps not infinite, list. If a man speaks the truth, then, his utterance also falls into one of these narrower classes; but just by knowing that he spoke the truth, we do not know *what* particular illocutionary force his utterance had.

More or less following Austin, we may then distinguish at least three categories under which our characterizations of a speech act may fall. First, we may describe it in terms of an intention or consequence that lies beyond the domain of language entirely, in the sense that the speech act was performed for the sake of that consequence, or at any rate had that consequence, but the description does not entail that the act involved speech. For example: he acted with the intention of getting Gertrude to move out of the path of danger (or, his act had that consequence).

Secondly, we may describe the act in terms of intentions specific to the issuance of a particular warning (or assertion, or promise). For example: he informed Gertrude that a train was approaching (with the intention of getting Gertrude to move out of the path of danger). For *this* description to apply, the speaker must, of course, have the intention of communicating by the use of language (and he must have succeeded). It also must be the case that he had some specifically linguistic intention or other of the sort next to be mentioned. But if all we know is that he informed Gertrude that a train was approaching, we do not know what his words were, and therefore do not know his specific linguistic intentions.

Thirdly, we may describe his action in terms of his actual words and the intentions necessary to uttering a particular sentence with shared truth conditions as an act of communication. For example: he spoke the words "A train is approaching" knowing that Gertrude knew that this sentence was true if and only if a train was at that moment approaching; by doing this he informed her that a train was approaching; and in doing this he intended to get Gertrude to move out of the path of danger.

I argued in my first lecture that the concepts applicable to specifically linguistic acts—the concepts I have just put on the third level of description—cannot be analyzed completely in terms of the concepts drawn from the first two levels. The concepts of what words mean as used, of a linguistic act, are *irreducible*—not, I hope it is now clear, in the sense of occurring in isolation from further intentions; not in the sense that we could detect or interpret them, or fully explain them, out of relation to further communicative intentions—but irreducible in the old-fashioned sense of not being *explicitly definable* (and hence theoretically eliminable) in terms of intentions (concepts) not specifically linguistic.

The second level does not yield to the first either. But perhaps the second level could be reduced to the first and the third together, though I do not believe anyone has succeeded in doing it. (An example would be to define assertion in terms of non-illocutionary concepts, such as non-linguistic intentions, *and* the concept of linguistic meaning.)

A theory of truth as I envision it accepts as unanalyzed the concept of speaking the truth, and constructs a theory for it which yields specific answers about what all the sentences of a language mean. To say the concept is unanalyzed does not mean we cannot do a great deal to elucidate the idea and relate it to others; a theory of truth does this in one direction; the study of illocutionary intentions does it in another.

The problem before us is this: given a theory of truth for the speech of someone else, how can we tell that the theory is correct? To answer this question is, as I said, to explain, to a depth that depends on the concepts that are taken as unanalyzed, how communication by language is possible. We know, or have decided, that a theory is adequate only if, using finite means, it entails a T-sentence for every sentence of the language under study. So we could test a theory by testing whether its consequences included the appropriate T-sentences; of course we cannot test for *all* T-sentences, since they are infinite in number, but we could test the theory, as any theory is tested, by sampling its consequences.

The trouble is that we have characterized a T-sentence by saying it has this form:

$$s \text{ is true (for p at t)} \leftrightarrow \ldots p \ldots t \ldots$$

where *s* is replaced by a preferred description of a sentence, and the dots are replaced by a sentence that "translates" or anyway "gives the truth condition" of *s*. But if we do not know what *s* means, how can we tell a T-sentence when we see one? How can we even tell it is *true*?

Actually, it *is* enough if we can tell when a sentence with the form of a T-sentence is true, as I shall argue presently. So if I am right, we can test a theory of truth if we can tell when a sentence of the form "*s* is true $\leftrightarrow$ p" is simply true (when relativized, as usual, to a speaker and a time). But how can we do this? Suppose the theory entails "'Es regnet' is true (in Carl's language) for a speaker at a time iff it is raining near the speaker at the time he speaks." We would have a start on telling whether this was true if we knew that "Es regnet" was true (in Carl's language) at a particular time and place, and that it was raining at that time and place. Now, however, we seem to have *two* problems: we need to know what "Es regnet" means in Carl's language, and when it *really* is raining! Starting out this way, we should have to know the objective truth of every one of our own sentences in order to arrive at a theory of truth for Carl's language.

At this point I suggest a double compromise. I propose, on the left, to accept Carl's own opinion, and on the right, mine, in the following sense: If, at a time and place I believe it is raining, Carl assents to the sentence "Es regnet," I shall count this in favor of the theory. Carl may think it is raining, and it may not; I may think it is raining, and it may not. Those are perturbations that cannot be expected to cancel one another out, but they are perturbations we can, and indeed must, ignore at the first stage of theory building. (Consider them errors in measurement.)

Of course, I do not suppose at the start that I can tell that Carl believes it is raining; what I do suppose I can tell is that he *accepts* the sentence "Es regnet" as a bit of his language. Since the concept of acceptance of a sentence forms the evidential base for my entire theory of meaning, I should say something more about it. On the one hand, it is a concept that is explicitly intensional, non-behavioristic, and has built into it the notion of a specifically linguistic response, intention, or attitude. On the other hand, its use by no means begs the problem of a theory of meaning, for it does not involve the concept of *what* a person, or an utterance, means, or of what a sentence, when uttered on an occasion, means. My entire project may indeed now be described as: constructing a theory that specifies *what* a sentence expresses for a speaker, given as evidence what sentences he believes express truths. There is a double advance. We begin by knowing only whether the speaker holds a sentence of his to express a truth, and we end by knowing under what conditions it really expresses a truth, also *what* truth it expresses for him.

How can we ascertain, when we do not understand the words of a speaker, when he holds a sentence to express a truth (relative to a speaker)? I don't think there is any *formula*, or simple test. If we can tell honest assertion when we meet it, and we often can, that provides important cases. (Luckily, or more than luckily, parents and others teaching children, and informants working with linguists, are supposed to specialize, at first, in honest assertion.) Dishonest assertion, if we can spot it, works as well. Dishonest assertion that we do not identify can also put us on the right track if the conditions are such as to deceive us about the objective truth. Other attitudes than assent can tip us off as to whether a speaker holds a sentence to express a truth: if we can tell that a speaker wonders whether a sentence is true, wants it to be true, wants us to make it true, expects it to be true, or intends to make it true, then we have some more evidence as to whether he holds a sentence to be true. As a body of theory begins to develop, considerations of coherence suggest that some attributions of assent to sentences confirm others. Coherence, and success of theory, may also lead to retrospective amendments to the first crude attributions of assent.

So far it is not easy to see how the evidence can suffice to discriminate between an intuitively satisfactory theory and a grotesquely wrong one. For we would seem to be in danger of accepting as a T-sentence any sentence that pairs off a sentence I believe to be true with any sentence to which the other assents. We must ask what disallows the absurdities.

Acceptance of a sentence is not a speech act but an attitude (which may be, but generally is not, evinced by a speech act); at a given moment, a speaker does or does not have this attitude toward every sentence of his language. Since we must treat his sentences as unlimited in number, there is no obvious way for a finite theory of truth to pair each sentence which the other accepts with an arbitrary sentence I know to be true, let us say "2 + 1 ≠ 2." There must be a *method* in the matching.

Not only must there be a method, but it can only be a method with the formal features of a T-theory. To appreciate the power of this restraint, imagine a language like English in every respect except spelling and pronunciation—for example, Dahdit, which is English in Morse code. Then it is easy to produce a formula for generating correct T-sentences, supposing that both speakers agree, in the obvious sense, on what is true. The formula is: to get a T-sentence, write a description of a sentence of Dahdit followed by "is true if and only if" followed by the English sentence got by turning Morse code into our alphabet. The trouble is that this theory is not a theory that satisfies Convention T—it is not a T-theory. The reason is clear: it does not give a finite set of axioms (which in a T-theory give a *semantic analysis* of the language) which entail the T-sentence; it simply gives syntactic criteria for producing the infinite set of T-sentences directly.

The simple ability to translate another man's language into ours does not go to the root of our ability to understand his language: only a theory of truth does that. What might obscure this point is that if we have a theory of truth for our own language, and a mechanical (i.e., purely syntactic) way of translating another language into ours, these two devices may be merged in an obvious way to form a theory of truth for the other language couched in ours. So it might be said: if I can translate, by no matter how blind a method (as I do French into English, say), *and* I understand my own language (which by definition I must), then I understand the foreign language. This is true. We are merely trying to make explicit what it is to understand a language: there cannot be a difference in kind between understanding our own language as an instrument of communication, and understanding another.

A theory of truth must discover a semantically tractable structure in its object language, and the only such structure we know or can use is the one that can be abstracted from our own language. At the moment, what we understand of *it* amounts, I have argued, to quantificational structure, though it is far from obvious that this is, or must be, the last word. That quantificational structure suffices for English is a hypothesis, to be tested by how well it does in competition with alternative hypotheses. That the structure which suits English suits another language is *not* a hypothesis because it could not, in the nature of the case, have an alternative. A failure to interpret another language in terms of the structure that fits ours is simply a failure to interpret the other language; it cannot be construed as evidence that the other language has a *different* structure.

One sees how a theory of truth might begin to be constructed from the materials at hand. We may imagine the theorist finding a syntactic operation on a pair of sentences of *Alien* such that the *Other* (our informant) assents to the result of that operation on two sentences if and only if he assents to each of the sentences alone. The theorist then puts a clause into his growing recursive theory of truth, saying that a sentence formed from two others by the given operation is true if and only if each of the original sentences is true. And so on for other truth functions.

I argued in my second lecture that a T-theory for English must treat its quantificational structure along more or less standard lines. So our theorist will hunt for an operation on any of a class of (syntactically specified) sentences that yields always the same sentence (call it E) and such that the *Other* assents to E if he assents to any sentence in the class; and if he assents to E, there is usually one in the class he assents to. The theorist will suppose he has identified the operation of existential generalization. An analogous method works for universal quantification. The *evidence* cannot prove to him that it is genuine (what Quine calls *ontic*) quantification rather than substitutional quantification that he has discovered; but I urged before that this is not a choice open to the theorist because substitutional quantification does not meet the standards of Convention T.

At this point the theorist will have projected the whole abstract pattern of quantification theory on the *Other*, and with it a *logic*, for the theory will entail that if some sentences of *Alien* are true, others must be. This can hardly be regarded as taking an unjustifiably charitable view of the rationality of the *Other*. As Quine points out, in the early stages of theory building, if a hypothesis makes the *Other* inconsistent, this discredits the hypothesis rather than the *Other*. We must have a well-verified theory going before we can make sense of attributions of error or inconsistency.

Now I hark back once more to our discussion, in the second lecture, of truth and ontology: in that discussion, it became clear that a theory of quantification needed something like the concept of *satisfaction* in the metalanguage. Satisfaction, you will remember, is a relation between sentences, open or closed, and sequences of entities. If I am right, the theorist, in reading quantificational structure into the *Other*'s tongue, will perforce have recourse to satisfaction (or a variant device) in constructing his theory and will therefore saddle the *Other* with his own ontology, along with a system of singular terms and predicates, and the machinery of identity. Endowing the *Other* with one's own ontology is inevitable once essential use is made of satisfaction, since the entities satisfaction relates to the sentences and predicates of *Alien* must be the entities to which the theory-maker can refer, and over which *he* can quantify.

In general outline, *Alien* begins to seem disappointingly familiar. Yet we have so far said little that would suggest where to start in giving the truth conditions for sentences in which we have identified no analogues of logical constants: the structure we can reproduce is that of quantificational logic. This cannot leave us totally in the dark about the structure of the simplest sentences, since predicates can be told from singular terms, and the number of places in a predicate can be determined. Still, how can we determine whether the *Other*'s sentence "Gavagai" is true if and only if there is a rabbit, *or* if and only if there is a warthog? The important clue lies in the relativization of truth to a time and a speaker. Relativized, T-sentences become universal *laws* saying that a sentence is true for any speaker at any time if certain conditions, that mention time and speaker, hold. We have been using, as the best evidence we can have to start with that a sentence *is* true in a person's language, the fact that he *holds* it to be true; now we see that of course this must be relativized to read: our evidence that a sentence is true in *Alien relative to a speaker and a time* is that the *Other* holds it to be true, relative to that speaker and at that time. Let us consider only the simplest case, where the speaker concerned is the *Other* himself, and the time of truth is the time the *Other* accepts the sentence as true. And suppose the *Other* is Carl again, with his sentence "Es regnet." And now, we notice that Carl accepts this sentence as true, with himself as speaker, when and only when—well, what? His feet are wet; or the streets glisten in his vicinity; or he hunts for his umbrella? Since a relativized T-sentence is a universal law, we can test it endlessly, and the more we test, the more probable it becomes that we will fix on: "Es regnet" is true in Carl's language relative to a speaker s and a time t if and only if it is raining in the vicinity of s at t; for what I have noticed, of course, is that Carl assents to "Es regnet" when and only when it is raining in his vicinity. By taking advantage of the sensitive correlations between linguistic assent and what goes on in the world, sentences with *indexical* elements greatly narrow the range of possible theories of their truth conditions. These limitations reverberate through the theory as a whole by way of the connections dictated by quantificational structure.

It does not seem plausible that the hopeful theorist will find a theory of truth for the *Other* that has the *Other* assenting to a sentence exactly when, according to the theory, that sentence is true. Starting with a small sample of the *Other*'s utterances, a theory might be found; but we must expect the honeymoon to be brief.

Not being able to find a workable theory that puts theorist and subject in perfect accord must be regarded by the theorist as evidence that either he, or his subject, is in error about something. But how can he decide which one? I think there is no *single* principle that decides in general. Various considerations will help, however. For example, if the theory-builder has fixed on some sentence of the *Other* as translating "I believe that" or "I intend to make it the case that" or "I hope that" or "I command that," then the theorist is bound to suppose that in almost every case, if the *Other* assents, the sentence is true. The theorist must assume the *Other* is more apt to assent to a false sentence about how things *are* than how they *seem* (and that he himself is more apt to be wrong about how things are than how they seem). The *Other* may be expected to err more often about what is distant than what is near, what is invisible than what is seen, what is observed under unfavorable circumstances—and so on.

I have been concentrating on the unreal situation in which one person is trying to understand the speech of *one* other; for that assumption sharpens issues. In the more natural case where the theorist has a speech *community* to study, his principles and method remain the same, but the choice between alternative theories is made easier. For the theorist, a speech community is a group to whom the same theory applies reasonably well. Where with one speaker to observe, only very general considerations could guide the choice between a theory that located a difference of opinion in one place rather than a theory that located it in another, a *number* of speakers might settle the matter by agreeing among themselves in assenting to some sentences and failing to agree on others. The shrewd theorist will pick a theory that makes the majority of speakers of *Alien* right—a point that might alternatively be put: agreement among speakers in assenting to a sentence spells a feature of language, divergence of assent spells disagreement about the world. (This does not distinguish between agreed synthetic truths and analytic.)

Of course, choosing a single theory for a number of speakers—counting them, that is, as speakers of the same language—is not only a necessary convenience. It is objectively justified, for the fact that the same theory works reasonably well to account for the speech behavior of a number of people is powerful evidence that they are each assuming a *homophonic* theory for one another—a theory that assigns the same truth conditions to the sentences of someone else as to the same sentences of one's own.

In constructing a theory of truth for an alien tongue, the general policy, I have suggested, is *charity*: we should choose a theory that makes the speaker, or the speakers, of that tongue wrong as little as possible—by our own lights, of course, since we have no others to go by. "Wrong as little as possible" is pretty vague, and must be interpreted in terms of our remarks on plausible error.

Here is a question that I now think must be answered: Is charity enough? It might well seem that it is not, for the following reason. Our basic evidence for constructing a theory is acceptance of a sentence. Acceptance of a sentence is, from the acceptor's point of view, the product of two elements, what the sentence *means*, and his own state of belief or knowledge. The task of the theory-builder is to sort these elements out, to the extent necessary for a theory of meaning. By being charitable, the theorist has simply opted for an overall theory that makes the *Other* as knowing and consistent as possible. What can justify such generosity? Why may it not be the case that the *Other* is dead wrong about many things—something the theorist could articulate only by choosing a less charitable theory? In a word, charity guarantees *coherence* on the part of the *Other*, but how can we pretend it must lead to understanding? When speakers of *Alien* are included, the problem becomes: why couldn't *all* speakers of *Alien* be radically mistaken? But put this way, it begins to be clear why the problem is not real.

We do not need an army to make the point, however: really massive misunderstanding cannot occur even in the two-person case. By misunderstanding I do not mean misreading only the words of another: of course there is no reason why I cannot arrive at a ridiculous scheme of translation. By misunderstanding I mean placing a consistent interpretation on his speech that leads me to attribute to him what I take to be vast error.

Suppose first this extreme case: the small nod with which the person I am trying to understand begins each utterance, I interpret as denial. And now, a cloud passes over the face of the sun; at this moment my friend says what I take to express his belief that a cloud is *not* passing before the sun. I'm surprised, but not astonished: perhaps he made a mistake. As the sun comes out, he seems to me to compound his error. He also denies, or so I make him out, that there is a tree before us, though I plainly see there is. Further remarks he makes bring out—supposing I interpret him correctly—that he does not believe that clouds are made of water vapor, nor that they occupy the sky, nor that they ever look like whales. For that matter, he apparently does not believe there *are* any clouds, or trees, or any sun.

Somewhere long before this it must dawn on me that his words do not mean what I took them to mean, nor *can* he have all the beliefs my system of interpretation foisted on him. This is not because my theory of his meanings is *unlikely* to be true; at a point soon reached, it is an unintelligible theory. The pattern of sentences to which my companion assents is all my evidence for what he means by those sentences, *and* for what he believes. Each time I take him as not accepting a sentence of his to which I have assigned truth conditions that would, I think, make it a true sentence, I subtract something from the base of agreement on which I must depend in making sense of his utterances, and of him. I can have him wrong about the cloud, but only if I have him agree that clouds occupy the sky, can look like whales, can eclipse the sun. More disagreement irresistibly invites the question, disagreement *about what*?

The principle is simple. A limit is placed on the extent of disagreement or misinterpretation by the fact that as disagreement increases, intelligibility decreases. A sharp difference of opinion is possible only between people who can take for granted a wide range of shared belief.

The point comes across whether one thinks in terms of constructing a theory of meaning for the *Other* or in terms of inferring, from his speech behavior, his scheme of belief. Seen the first way, our reasoning shows that mistakes across the board about what someone else means cannot be reconciled with any intelligible pattern of acceptance of sentences; seen the second way, the argument should convince us that there is no way to attribute to others really wholesale divergences from our own doctrines, for each supposed divergence undermines the sense we can make of the next attribution, whether divergent or not. That we can see the point in these two ways is no accident, for both trace back to the fact that the same body of evidence—the pattern of sentences in his own language which a speaker accepts—must serve for each hearer the double purpose of constructing a theory of meaning *and* a theory of belief for the speaker.

Not that these two studies cannot be pursued independently; to some extent they can. Having settled on a theory, satisfactory up to now, of what another means by his words, I can use his observed or inferred acceptances as evidence for his beliefs. But when this strategy leads me to attribute unintelligible patterns of beliefs to the speaker, I must change my theory or give up trying to make sense of what he says and thinks. And long before this happens, a shift in my theory of his meanings may make for a more plausible total theory than the attribution of a mind-shattering absurdity.

For much the same reason that it is not possible to go wholly wrong in the interpretation of the thoughts and utterances of others, it is also not possible for anyone to be radically mistaken about how things are. Imagine for a moment that the person whose speech and worldview I am trying to grasp is omniscient; every sentence to which he assents is true (in his language). I cannot know that this is the case (excluding revelation), even if he tells me it is, so I attack the problem of translation and interpretation as usual. And as usual, I get it right enough, of necessity. Getting it right means only constructing a theory of his talk so that a minimum of sentences assented to by him are assigned truth conditions that would make those sentences false the way I see things. Bearing in mind the secret that he assents only to the true, we see that any acceptable theory will be one that makes most of my beliefs true also. Yet this result is quite independent of any special knowledge of mine.

We really do not need the myth of the omniscient informant to appreciate the contradiction in the idea of comprehensive error. Perhaps I am wrong about yonder cloud. But then I cannot *also* be wrong about what clouds are made of, where they usually appear, what they look like, and so on; a few such mistakes take the starch out of the first. The foundation of error is truth, simply because truth is the basis of meaning.

This one-sentence transcendental refutation of all skepticism, because it is perfectly general, and in application rests on matters of degree, yields no interesting answer to particular skeptical doubts. At best it provides the principle that must underlie the strategy of reply. But the present purpose requires nothing specific. Our problem was to understand how, given that undeciphered linguistic responses are a vector of the forces of language and of doctrine, communication is possible. This problem is solved when we recognize that though any particular portion of doctrine may be wrong, and may not be shared, global error and massive misunderstanding are, in the nature of the case, excluded.

I find that like some other metaphysicians I am given to talking about "Our Conceptual Scheme" and the project of delineating its major structural features. If what I have been saying is right, it would be as correct to describe such a project as that of delineating the major structural features of reality. And it would be *less* misleading, since phrases like "Our Conceptual Scheme" inevitably suggest that there might be others, and this, I have been arguing, is a mistake. There cannot be seriously different total sets of beliefs. It follows that it cannot be a difference between *languages* that *one* is geared to *one* conceptual scheme, and another to another. By the same token, I think there is no understanding the idea that ontology is relative to a language.

There remains, however, another sort of relativity about which I have so far said nothing. Let me introduce it through an analogy with the ordinary measurement of temperature. The numbers assigned to a body as a measure of its temperature convey information only when we know what has been selected as a starting point (or zero) and what has been chosen as the unit of measurement. So, to know that the air temperature is 57 tells us nothing unless we know that this number gives the temperature on the Fahrenheit, or Centigrade, or another, scale. But though individual numbers are relative to a system of measurement, there are many facts of measurement that are not. For example, if B is midway in temperature between A and C, it is so on *any* scale; similarly, if the difference in temperature between A and B is twice the difference in temperature between C and D. These latter facts may be called *invariants* of temperature—unlike assignments of numbers, they are not relative to an arbitrary scheme or system. I call the system, for example Centigrade or Fahrenheit, *arbitrary* because there is no aspect of what is being measured that is captured by one scheme and not the other; the two schemes do not differ in the information they convey.

Suppose that two different, but equally satisfactory, theories of truth could be constructed for the same language. The common constraints are, *first* (as I have suggested), that sentences to which speakers assent be assigned truth conditions that make those sentences true (by our own lights, and as tempered by considerations of plausible error); and, *second*, that the theory satisfy the formal constraints implied by Convention T (chiefly that there be a finite number of non-logical axioms, and no semantic primitives not recursively characterized). The question is, what is invariant over such equally satisfactory (as we assume) theories? The short answer is: *meaning*—that was, anyway, the intent. But this is like saying that what is invariant as between schemes for measuring temperature is temperature. In the case of temperature we can give a precise answer: everything is invariant that is left intact by all linear transformations of the systems of numbers, that is to say, the number assignments are unique up to a linear transformation (which is a transformation that may move the zero point or change the unit).

At this stage of the science we cannot expect so precise an answer for theories of truth. But one *relatively* clear *question* is: to what extent is ontology invariant? Can equally satisfactory theories of truth explain the truth of the same sentences by appeal to different ontologies? I think we must expect to find a difference between objects like mountains, mice, marriages, and murders on the one hand, and abstract entities such as numbers on the other. It seems to me that bearing in mind the enormous constraints on the truth conditions of sentences with demonstrative or indexical expressions, the only variations possible will be relatively detailed—they will concern the existence of particular entities, or relatively small classes of entities, like witches, elves, and werewolves. In the case of numbers, however, there would seem to be an infinity of different sets of entities, each of which, aside from sentences whose truth hardly matters to us, do exactly as well in organizing the truths about numbers. Perhaps there are cases intermediate between the mice and numbers, for example neutrons or diseases.

[If these remarks are right, then it would seem, at least in the case of mathematical sentences, that we cannot say what they are about. If this question arises about the ontology of others, it arises equally about our own. But if each of two quite different ontologies explains all we say in some domain exactly as well as the other, this is to say we can find no differences between those ontologies whatsoever. In what sense, then, are they *two*?]

The pursuit of these matters would take us beyond the scope of my present subject. To show how language is possible it is enough to demonstrate that a great deal is invariant from theory to theory of truth; to investigate in more detail the question *what* is invariant belongs to metaphysics and physics.

The study of invariance is the study of significant pattern and structure under various systematic forms of representation. What sets apart the approach to the concept of linguistic meaning that I have been advocating and exploring is its rejection of the idea that we can work our way into a language by first grasping the meanings of particular words, then assembling these into sentences, then grouping and relating the sentences. The piecemeal or building-blocks approach is no better in the guise of the idea that first we must grasp the import of certain sentences—those closest to experience in some way, perhaps—and then build a structure on this base.

The seamless character of thought and meaning prevents us from making sense of fragments until we have a comprehensive theory in which the fragments have been assigned a role. We have no alternative to the holistic approach to language. There is no need to reject the concepts of meaning, proposition, synonymy, and analyticity to appreciate why they cannot play a part in building a theory of meaning; it is simply that they *presuppose* a theory, and so cannot found it.

If we look for a foundation elsewhere, in epistemology, I think again the result can only be to encourage skepticism.

The only basis for a theory of meaning is the whole fabric of belief as evinced in a system of behavior. This works because each of us cannot help being right enough about the world to explain why the total pattern of his acceptance, as given structure and expression in a theory of truth, must match, nearly enough, the total pattern of each *Other.*

Selected Bibliography

Amoretti, Maria and Nicla Vassalo (eds), 2009, *Knowledge, Language, and Interpretation: On the Philosophy of Donald Davidson*, Frankfurt-Heusenstamm: Ontos Verlag.

Baghramian, Maria (ed.), 2013, *Donald Davidson: Life and Words*, London: Routledge.

Carnap, Rudolf, 1947, *Meaning and Necessity: A Study in Semantics and Modal Logic*, Chicago: University of Chicago Press.

Church, Alonzo, 1956, *Introduction to Mathematical Logic* (vol. 1), Princeton: Princeton University Press.

Davidson, Donald, 1963, "Actions, Reasons, and Causes," *Journal of Philosophy* 60(23), pp. 685–700. Reprinted in Davidson (1980), pp. 3–19.

Davidson, Donald, 1967, "Reply to Castañeda on Agent and Patient" in Nicholas Rescher (ed.) *The Logic of Decision and Action*, pp. 117–118. Reprinted in Davidson (1980), pp. 125–126.

Davidson, Donald, 1967, "The Logical Form of Action Sentences," in Nicholas Rescher (ed.) *The Logic of Decision and Action*, pp. 81–95. Reprinted in Davidson (1980), pp. 105–122.

Davidson, Donald, 1967, "Truth and Meaning," *Synthese* 17, pp. 304–23. Reprinted in Davidson (1984), pp. 17–36.

Davidson, Donald, 1968, "On Saying That," *Synthese* 19, 130–146. Reprinted in Davidson (1984), pp. 93–108.

Davidson, Donald, 1969, "True to the Facts," *Journal of Philosophy* 66(21), pp. 748–64. Reprinted in Davidson (1984), pp. 37–54.

Davidson, Donald, 1970, "Reply to Cargyle," *Inquiry* 13, pp. 140–148 (published under the title "Action and Reaction"). Reprinted in Davidson (1980), pp. 137–146.

Davidson, Donald, 1970, "Semantics for Natural Languages," in *Linguaggi nella Società e nella Tecnica*, Milan: Edizioni di Comunità. Reprinted in Davidson (1984), pp. 55–64.

Davidson, Donald, 1973, "In Defense of Convention T," in Hughes Leblanc (ed.) *Truth, Syntax, and Modality: Proceedings of the Temple University Conference on Alternative Semantic Studies in Logic and the Foundations of Mathematics* (vol. 68), Amsterdam: North-Holland Publishing Company. Reprinted in Davidson (1984), pp. 65–75.

Davidson, Donald, 1973, "Radical Interpretation," *Dialectica* 27, pp. 313–28. Reprinted in Davidson (1984), pp. 125–140.

Davidson, Donald, 1974, "On the Very Idea of a Conceptual Scheme," *Proceedings and Addresses of the American Philosophical Association* 47, pp. 5–20. Reprinted in Davidson (1984), pp. 183–198.

Davidson, Donald, 1976, "Reply to Foster," in Gareth Evans and John McDowell (eds) *Truth and Meaning: Essays in Semantics*, pp. 33–41. Reprinted in Davidson (1984), pp. 171–179.

Davidson, Donald, 1977, "The Method of Truth in Metaphysics," in P.A. French, T.E. Uehling, Jr., and H.K. Wettstein (eds) *Midwest Studies in Philosophy* (vol. 2), pp. 244–254. Reprinted in Davidson (1984), pp. 199–214.

Davidson, Donald, 1979, "Moods and Performances," in A. Margalit (ed.) *Meaning and Use*, Dordrecht: D. Reidel Publishing Company, pp. 9–20. Reprinted in Davidson (1984), pp. 109–121.

Davidson, Donald, 1979, "Quotation," *Theory and Decision* 11, pp. 27–40. Reprinted in Davidson (1984), pp. 79–92.

Davidson, Donald, 1980, *Essays on Actions and Events*, Oxford: Clarendon Press.

Davidson, Donald, 1984, "Communication and Convention," *Synthese* 59(1): 3–17. Reprinted in Davidson (1984), pp. 265–280.

Davidson, Donald, 1984, *Inquiries into Truth and Interpretation*, Oxford: Clarendon Press.

Evnine, Simon, 1991, *Donald Davidson*, Cambridge: Polity Press.

Fodor, Jerry and Ernest Lepore, 1992, *Holism: A Shopper's Guide*, Oxford: Blackwell.

Geach, Peter, 1957, *Mental Acts: Their Content and Their Objects*, London: Routlege and Kegan Paul.

Geach, Peter, 1963, "Quantification Theory and the Problem of Identifying Objects of Reference," *Acta Philosophia Fennica* 16, pp. 41–52.

Gluer, K., 1993, *Donald Davidson zur Einführung*, Hamburg: Junius Verlag.

Gluer, K., 2011, *Donald Davidson: A Short Introduction*, New York: Oxford University Press.

Hahn, Lewis Edwin (ed.), 1999, *The Philosophy of Donald Davidson*, Library of Living Philosophers (vol 27), Chicago: Open Court.

Kotatko, Petr, Peter Pagin, and Gabriel Segal (eds), 2001, *Interpreting Davidson*, Stanford: CSLI Publications.

Lepore, Ernie (ed.), 1986, *Truth and Interpretation: Perspectives on the Philosophy of Donald Davidson*, Oxford: Basil Blackwell.

Lepore, Ernie and Kirk Ludwig, 2006, *Donald Davidson: Meaning, Truth, Language and Reality*, Oxford: Clarendon Press.

Lepore, Ernie and Kirk Ludwig, 2007, *Donald Davidson's Truth-Theoretic Semantics*, Oxford: Clarendon Press.

Lepore, Ernie and Kirk Ludwig (eds), 2013, *A Companion to Donald Davidson*, Oxford: Wiley-Blackwell.

Lepore, Ernie and Brian McLaughlin (eds), 1985, *Actions and Events: Perspectives on the Philosophy of Donald Davidson*, Oxford: Basil Blackwell.

Ludwig, Kirk (ed.), 2003, *Donald Davidson*, New York: Cambridge University Press.

Malpas, Jeff, 1992, *Donald Davidson and the Mirror of Meaning*, Cambridge: Cambridge University Press.

Malpas, Jeff (ed.), 2011, *Dialogues with Davidson: Acting, Interpreting, Understanding*, Cambridge, Mass.: The MIT Press.

Mates, Benson, 1965, *Elementary Logic*, Oxford: Oxford University Press.

Myers, Robert and Claudine Verheggen, 2016, *Donald Davidson's Triangulation Argument: A Philosophical Inquiry*, London: Routledge.

Preyer, Gerhard (ed.), 2012, *Donald Davidson on Truth, Meaning, and the Mental*, Oxford: Oxford University Press.

Preyer, Gerhard, Frank Siebelt, and Alexander Ulfig (eds.), 1994, *Language, Mind and Epistemology*, Dordrecht: Kluwer.

Quine, W.V., 1940, *Mathematical Logic*, Cambridge: Harvard University Press.

Quine, W.V., 1950, *Methods of Logic*, New York: Henry Holt and Co.

Quine, W.V., 1953, *From a Logical Point of View*, Cambridge, Mass.: Harvard University Press.

Quine, W.V., 1960, *Word and Object*, Cambridge, Mass.: The MIT Press.

Ramberg, Bjorn, 1989, *Donald Davidson's Philosophy of Language: An Introduction*, Oxford: Basil Blackwell.

Reichenbach, Hans, 1947, *Elements of Symbolic Logic*, New York: Macmillan.

Ross, John R., 1970, "Metalinguistic Anaphora," *Linguistic Inquiry*, 1(2), p. 273.

Stoecker, Ralf (ed.), 1993, *Reflecting Davidson*, Berlin: W. de Gruyter.

Tarski, Alfred, 1956, "The Concept of Truth in Formalized Languages," in *Logic, Semantics, Metamathematics*, Oxford: Clarendon Press, pp. 159–62.

Verheggen, Claudine (ed.), 2017, *Wittgenstein and Davidson on Thought, Language, and Action*, Cambridge: Cambridge University Press.

Vermazen, B. and M. Hintikka, 1985, *Essays on Davidson: Actions and Events*, Oxford: Clarendon Press.

Zeglen, Ursula M. (ed.), 1991, *Donald Davidson: Truth, Meaning and Knowledge*, London: Routledge.

Index

For the benefit of digital users, indexed terms that span two pages (e.g., 52–53) may, on occasion, appear on only one of those pages.

.

9 780198 842491